Social Policy in a
Non-Democratic Regime

Social Policy in a Non-Democratic Regime

The Case of Public Housing in Brazil

Gil Shidlo

Westview Press
BOULDER, SAN FRANCISCO, & OXFORD

HD
7323
528
553
1990

This Westview softcover edition is printed on acid-free paper and bound in library-quality, coated covers that carry the highest rating of the National Association of State Textbook Administrators, in consultation with the Association of American Publishers and the Book Manufacturers' Institute.

Published in 1990 in the United States of America by Westview Press, Inc., 5500 Central Avenue, Boulder, Colorado 80301, and in the United Kingdom by Westview Press, Inc., 36 Lonsdale Road, Summertown, Oxford OX2 7EW

Library of Congress Cataloging-in-Publication Data
Shidlo, Gil, 1956–
  Social policy in a non-democratic regime: the case of public
housing in Brazil/Gil Shidlo.
    p. cm.
  Includes bibliographical references.
  Includes index.
  ISBN 0-8133-7866-4
  1. Housing policy—Brazil—São Paulo. 2. Housing policy—Brazil—
São Paulo—Finance. 3. Itaquera (São Paulo, Brazil)—Social
conditions. 4. Itaquera (São Paulo, Brazil)—Economic conditions.
I. Title.
HD7323.S28S53 1990
363.5′8′098161—dc20   90-35990
                                                                                   CIP

Printed and bound in the United States of America

      The paper used in this publication meets the requirements
 ∞   of the American National Standard for Permanence of Paper
      for Printed Library Materials Z39.48-1984.

10   9   8   7   6   5   4   3   2   1

Contents

Tables and Figures

Abbreviations

All abbreviations and terms are explained in full in the text.

ABC	Heavily industrialized region of Sao Paulo state.
ACOMINAS	Large steel mill in Minas Gerais.
AID	Agency for International Development (USAID).
APE	Savings and Loans Association.
ARENA	National Renovating Alliance.
Autarquias	State Enterprises created during the Vargas regime.
BANESPA	State Bank of Sao Paulo.
BIRD	International Bank for Reconstruction & Development.
BNDE	National Bank for Economic Development.
BNH	National Housing Bank.
Castellista	Supporter of Castelo Branco.
CEAGESP	Sewage Company of Sao Paulo.
CECAP	The predecessor of CODESPAULO.
CEE's	State Saving Bank.
CEF	Federal Saving Bank—Caixa Economica Federal.
CEI	Special Inquiry Commission.
CGI	General Investigations Commissions.
CGT	General Labour Command.
CHISAM	BNH agency for Favela removal in Rio de Janeiro.
CNTI	National Confederation of Workers in Industry.
CODESPAULO	Housing Company of the State of Sao Paulo.
COHAB	State Housing Company.
CONTEC	National Confederation of Workers in Establishments of Credit.
COOPHAB	Housing Cooperatives.
coronelismo	Brazilian term for clientelistic politics.
Cortico(s)	Slum(s).
COSIPA	Sao Paulo state steel corporation.
CPI	Parliamentary Committee of Inquiry.
DASP	Administrative Department of Public Service.
DCI	Association of Christian Employers.

descompressao	Literally, decompression. Move toward less repressive forms of government and control.
desestatizacao	A process of reducing state control.
DNOCS	National Department of Anti-Drought Works.
Electrobras	State-owned and controlled electric power corporation.
Eletropaulo	Electricity corporation of Sao Paulo.
Embrioes	Small houses built by COHAB for ex-favelados.
EMPLASA	The Sao Paulo State Metropolitan Planning Company.
EMURB	Municipal Urban Development Company.
ESG	National Military College.
favela	Shanty town. Essentially an area of low-cost housing.
fazenda	An estate. Also treasury or finance, as in Ministro de Fazenda, Ministry of Finance.
FCP	Foundation for Popular Housing.
FEPASA	Sao Paulo Railway Corporation.
FGTS	Social security fund for employees.
filhotismo	Part of duty of political leader or patrao to look after the interests of his clients.
FIMACO	BNH program to finance production and acquisition of building materials.
FMP	Popular Mobilization Front.
FRN	Front of National Renovation.
GDP	Gross Domestic Product.
GEIPOT	The Brazilian Planning and Transport Enterprise.
getulismo	Political philosophy and policies of Getulio Vargas. Also getulista: supporter of Getulio Vargas.
GNP	Gross National Product.
GSP	Greater Sao Paulo.
IAPI	Institute of Pensions for Industry.
IBGE	Brazilian Institute of Geography & Statistics.
IBMEC	Brazilian Institute of the Capital Market.
ICM	Industrial Sales Tax.
INAMPS	National Social Security Institute.
INOCOOP	Institute for the Guidance of Cooperatives.
IPEA	Institute of Applied Social and Economic Research.
IPESP	Public Housing Finance Institute (pre-1964).
IPM	Military-Police Investigations.
IPT	Institute of Technology Research.

IUPERJ	Research Institute of the Rio de Janeiro University.
Latifundio	Very large holding of land.
MDB	Brazilian Democratic Movement.
Mineiro	A native of Minas Gerais.
Minifundo	Small rural property.
MSD	Democratic Trade Union Movement.
Municipio	Municipality. Administrative and political district.
ORTN	Index Linked Federal Treasury Bonds.
PAEG	Government Program for Economic Action.
Patrao	Patron, boss. Often political patron.
Paulista	A native of, or appertaining to, the state of Sao Paulo.
PCB	Brazilian Communist Party.
PCdoB	Communist Party of Brazil.
PDT	Democratic Labour Party.
Petrobras	State-owned and directed petroleum company.
Planasa	National Sanitation Program.
PLANHAP	National Plan for Popular Housing.
PMDI	Sao Paulo Metropolitan Plan for Integrated Development.
PRODAM	Municipality Data Processing Company.
PROSINDI	Trade Union Housing Program.
PRP	Sao Paulo Republican Party.
PSB	Brazilian Socialist Party.
PSD	Social Democratic Party.
PTB	Brazilian Labour Party.
RECON	BNH sub-program to finance building materials acquisition.
SABESP	Sao Paulo State Sanitation Company.
SAC	The Constant Amortization Scheme of Mortgage Repayment.
SAS	Statistical Analysis System.
SBPE	Brazilian System for Savings and Loans.
SCI	Real Estate Credit Company.
SERFHAU	Federal System of Housing and Urbanism.
SFH	Housing Finance System.
SFS	Sanitation Financing System.
SM	Minimum monthly salary.
SNI	National Information Service (Intelligence).
SP	Sao Paulo state.
SUDAM	Superintendency for the Development of the Amazonas.

SUDECO	Superintendency for the Development of the Centre-East.
SUDELPA	Superintendency for the Development of Fishing.
SUDENE	Superintendency for the Development of the North-East.
SUMOC	Superintendency of Money and Credit.
SUPRA	Superintendency of Agrarian Policy.
Tenentes	Young Military Officers.
UDN	National Democratic Union.
UPC	Standard Capital Unit (constant value for financial indexation).
USAID	United States Aid for International Development.
USIMINAS	Large state-funded Minas Gerais steel mill.

Acknowledgments

This book had its origins in my doctoral research at the London School of Economics. It developed more rapidly than expected thanks to the good will and collective efforts of various people and institutions who provided help and support—material, intellectual and moral—throughout four years at the LSE and two years at Tel Aviv University. I am most grateful to George Philip and Patrick Dunleavy, who have patiently read the many drafts and offered their comments and suggestions at various stages of this work. I would also like to thank Peter Dawson, who during my early days at the LSE as a research and MSc student, supervised, advised and above all encouraged my intentions to carry out research on developing countries. Henrique Rattner of the Fundacao Getulio Vargas provided me not only with technical support but also introduced me to the complex Brazilian bureaucracy. Gabriel Bolaffi, of the Faculty of Architecture and Urbanism at the University of Sao Paulo, made it possible for me to gain access to the otherwise restricted public housing agencies. I also extend my gratitude to the officials at COHAB/SP, CODESPAULO, INOCOOP and the BNH (in Rio de Janeiro and Sao Paulo) who spared precious time to be interviewed and supplied me with published and unpublished documents. The IPT (Sao Paulo Institute of Technological Research) provided the primary material on Itaquera and enabled me to use their computing facilities and process the data. Special thanks are due to Ros Mari Kaupatez. The friends we made in Sao Paulo, whose welcome and warmth surpassed all expectations, made a long stay more bearable. This project could not have been carried out without the moral and financial support of both my grandfather and my parents, who took a deep interest in my studies and encouraged me during difficult periods. A debt of thanks is also owed to the Publication Committee of the London School of Economics, especially P. C. Davis. Anthony Hall's comments were very valuable. Thanks are due to the Faculty of Social Sciences and the Department of Political Science at Tel Aviv University for financial help in preparing this work for publication. Finally, this study is dedicated to my wife, Sarah, who interrupted her studies to accompany me to Brazil and helped me in ways I cannot adequately acknowledge.

Gil Shidlo

1

Theoretical Approaches to Social Policy in Non-Democratic Regimes

Introduction

This book is about non-democratic regimes and social policy. During the last four decades military governments have predominated the political scene in Latin America, Asia, Africa and the Middle East. Since the nineteen fifties, the great majority of non-democratic countries have created organizations which plan and invest in social policy programs and projects which are known by various names in different countries. Most have produced five-year development plans which emphasize the need to invest in urbanization, housing, education, health and educational programs. The development of social programmes is an important policy objective of governments in non-democratic countries. It is imperative to realise that, in non-democratic regimes, governments are by far the most important agencies in these areas and can do much more than private enterprise can ever hope to achieve. Government initiative in this area can be judged from the fact that in the mid-1970s, 3.5 percent of all non-democratic countries' GNP was spent on public health and education expenditure. This is quite a superior performance relative to historical standards.

But this whole phenomena of public expenditure in non-democratic regimes raises some very interesting general questions. The first question to ask is: Why do non-democratic states need to spend a significant proportion of their budget on social services such as health, education, public housing, etc.? Another aspect of this problem is how far the limits of welfare are imposed by 'structural' limits of capitalism itself, or result from a more complex balance of forces. Military, non-competitive regimes are generally believed to have a tendency to spend more for national-security purposes and less on welfare provision. "The institutionalization of authoritarian rule does seem to require the support of a satisfied and unified military and the presence of a large

1

internal police apparatus for informational and security purposes."[1] In Western societies there has been a tendency to enlarge and make more comprehensive the range of social services and facilities covered by government. Why do military non-competitive regimes have tendencies similar to those of Western democracies where the state's economic expansion extends beyond that required by strictly economic considerations? Although we would have expected to have seen an increasing or at least a stable level of expenditure on the military in an authoritarian regime, it is suprising that expenditure on defence has actually had a declining trend in various non-democratic regimes (e.g. in Brazil and in Argentina). Rather, investment in the provision of social services, in absolute terms, has shown a large increase in the last twenty years. We would have also anticipated that the new non-democratic regime types, the bureaucratic-authoritarian (B-A) states identified by O'Donnell, would adopt a rational-comprehensive or 'technocratic' approach to social policies. On the contrary one of the main arguments developed throughout this book is that taking the case of urban social policy in Brazil it is possible to highlight the essential political nature of the policy process in non-democratic regimes.

We would also have expected that most of the non-democratic regimes would have pinned their hopes on the Chicago School of thought whose main representative is Milton Friedman. Stating it succinctly, like its counterpart in Chile, the economic policy of non-democratic governments' should have followed a monetarist ideology which assumes that high rates of capital accumulation and growth are achieved by reducing the role of the state to a minimum. This means that the state should exercise purely administrative and fiscal functions and transfer all productive and social welfare functions to the private sector. Most state subsidies, particularly those which favour the consumer, should have been removed. However instead of having seen the dismantling of state enterprises and agencies, as was the case in Chile in the mid-1970s, the vast majority of non-democratic states have increased their involvement in the economy. During the 1960s and 1970s the expansion of these states in the economy occurred both through the consolidation and growth of their various activities and through the creation of some new areas of government action such as public housing.

This book will try to analyse the logic behind social policy expenditure in non-democratic regimes by looking at the Brazilian case during the period of 1964 to 1985. It will also look at the new civilian government of Brazil, installed in March 1985, and demonstrate that authoritarianism and democracy are not radically distinct. In 1964 the Brazilian political system underwent a basic change. The military overthrew a civilian government which had suffered from instability and paralysis. Authoritarianism in uniform got the upper hand in Brazil after a long spell of sluggish growth, increasing inflation and political stalemate. The military claim, for a period of twenty one years, to act as the nation's arbiter was successfully reinforced as the political system evolved toward corporatism. Rather than depending on competition among political parties or intermittent pressures of a large number of interest groups, policy making was seen to be in the process of becoming a system of high-level bargaining and consultation between government officials and leading actors in the private economy. An institutionalized process of continuing negotiation among a small number of highly organized and centralized interest groups (especially workers, employers, and professional associations) and an equally well-organized government apparatus, replaced the erratic and ad hoc collaboration with the government. After the 1964 coup, interests that were once expressed through comparatively independent trade unions, were corporatively organized in such a way as to eliminate the possibility of local horizontal union federations across sectors. Certain aspects of the labour code were modified and controls were applied with full severity. The takeover of 400 unions, the introduction of the anti-strike law, the suspension of wage bargaining and the abolition of job security provisions effectively stifled resistance to the government's harsh economic policies. But the key to government control of the federations is a highly non-representative election procedure for federation leaders.

All these circumstances did in fact stabilize investment and led to significant industrial and urban growth without any major challenges to the new power-holders. It also seems that despite the authoritarian regime, the disciplining of powerful economic and political interests, the centralization of employers and workers associations, a fairly stable pattern of state public expenditure and investment in social programs had been maintained (see Table 1.1). The rapid growth in expenditure on the social services, certain infra-structure items and aid to private and state industries, together with the decline in the share absorbed by armaments are all clearly discernible not only in Brazil but in all advanced capitalist countries. The most striking feature is the extent to which the social services (including housing) have expanded continuously since the mid-1960s and today account for a third of public expenditure. Parallel with this expansion has been the ubiquitous decline in military spending in relative terms. Other major developments since 1964 have been a growth in infra-structure expenses and transport. When looking into the nature and distribution of public expenditure on the social services, or state social expenditure in Brazil, it is not enough to examine the latter merely as a share of total federal expenditure as the budget includes only resources which are financed by

TABLE 1.1   Trends in Federal Budget Outlays by Major Categories Fiscal
            Years/Categories

	Economic	Social	Military	Administrative	Total
1964	43	18	17	22	100
1967	27	14	22	37	100
1970	48	17	28	7	100
1972	35	19	40	6	100
1975	27	27	38	8	100
1977	28	35	31	6	100
1979	48	28	19	5	100
1982	54	23	18	5	100
1983	53	24	18	5	100
1984	49	27	19	5	100
1985	45	30	20	5	100

Notes:

Social Category includes - Ministries of Education and Culture; Health;
Welfare and Social Security; Labour; Interior.

Military Category includes - Ministry of the Army; Navy; Airforce.

Economic Category includes - Ministry of Agriculture; Industry and
Commerce; Transport; Communications; Energy and Mineral Resources.

Administrative Category includes - Ministry for Foreign Affairs

Presidency of the Republic; Treasury; Legislative and Judicial Powers;
Planning and General Coordination (during the period - 1968/74).

direct and indirect taxes. Thus, if we look at public enterprises which
are 'autonomous' (not financed by the Treasury) and are not included
in the above figures, we observe that expenditure on social services has
expanded even more (as a percentage of GNP). The National Health
Service (INAMPS), the National Housing Bank, and nearly all 400
state companies (e.g. PETROBRAS; EMBRAER; INGESA) are all part
of Brazil's extended public sector. When looking at government expenditures as a proportion of GDP in Brazil we note that they have stood

at an average of 20 percent since the post-World War II period (this refers to all levels of government) but this does not include public enterprises for which hardly any reliable figures are available. It is also necessary to analyse state and local governments' expenditures as they are major agencies for spending money on the social services.

One of the large gaps in our understanding of politics in non-democratic regimes is the need for studies to elucidate the structural, budgetary and institutional effects of military rule on social policy. Except for recent general books on Latin American economic policy-making by Gary Wynia and on public policy by S. Hughes and K. Mijeski this field has not attracted enough attention.[2] Both these books focus on the question of how governments make decisions. Although non-democratic regimes have been activist for several decades, it is important to note that no studies have been carried out on the role of military regimes vis-a-vis social policy programs.

State and Local Expenditures on Welfare

In contrast to the clear separation of revenue sources, the Brazilian federal law is vague when it comes to allocating responsibilities to the states and municipalities. Legally the states are allowed to engage in any activity not forbidden to them by the Federal Constitution. Theoretically this has given the states considerable freedom. But in practice, the lack of a strict delineation of functions has led to a situation in which a wide range of public services are provided by more than one level of government (see Table 1.2). All services are provided jointly, to some extent by the federal government. However, one can observe a tendency of several levels of governments to specialize in specific functional areas. In the area of social services both the state and local level specialize. Thus, in 1975 both the state and local levels were responsible for a significant amount of public expenditure in housing and urban services (99 percent), health and sanitation (50 percent) and education (75 percent). Municipal governments are intensively active in the area of social services (e.g., housing and urban services; primary education). A notable trend in the 1964–84 period has been the growth of the federal government as the major tax-collecting agent which increased its power in determining the use of funds transferred to local authorities.

We shall now seek to apply the analysis of public housing to the trends in state expenditure noted above. Public housing is a service which until the mid-1930s was left mainly to commercial and philanthropic agencies.[3] During the 1960s and 1970s the expansion of the state in Brazil's economy occurred both through the consolidation and

TABLE 1.2 Public Expenditures by Functions and Level of Government, 1975 (in million of US$)

Functional Categories	Federal	State	Municipal	Total
All Social Services	11309	4100	800	16209
Housing & Urban Services	9	200	400	609
Education	750	1900	170	2820
Health & Sanitation	1200	900	150	2250
Labour & Welfare	9350	1100	80	10530
Administrative Services	5100	2660	280	8040
Police	500	-	-	500
Defense & Foreign Affairs	1000	820	5	1825
Administration	3600	1840	275	5715
Economic Services	4900	2255	290	7445
Energy	370	475	-	845
Agriculture & Natural Resources	730	270	-	1000
Industry & Commerce	1500	210	20	1730
Transport & Communications	2300	1300	270	3870
Total	21309	9015	1370	31694

growth of its various activities and through the creation of some new areas of government action. Since the creation of the National Housing Bank in 1964 state involvement in housing provision has been enormous. Housing has been one of the areas of general personal consumption, along with education, in which successive governments for the past twenty years have been keenly concerned. Several million dwellings have been financed by the Federal Housing System since 1964. Over U.S. $10 billion were invested by the National Housing Bank up to 1975. Currently there are a wide variety of programs requiring direct public expenditure, including the provision of state and municipal housing, payments to trade union housing associations and state-financed mortgages.

Public subsidy of housing has been justified on a number of a grounds, including the promotion of social efficiency and the attainment of minimum standards. But it can be viewed as the response of the state to various economic and political factors. There are several reasons for greater state intervention in the Brazilian housing market. Public housing programs are essential because of technocratic necessity; because they further the development of the welfare state; because of the necessity to stimulate economic growth; because of their capacity for creating employment and because of fears that the 'favelas' (shanty-towns) might provide a breeding ground for subversion.

An Overview of Recent Literature

Literature on housing studies in Brazil results from a variety of analytical approaches. The bulk of studies in this specialized field is concentrated around three main topics: favelas; government housing policies; periphery housing tracts and self-built housing. During the 1960s and 1970s, Latin American research concentrated on sociological studies on the 'favelas'. This occurred at a time when the so called 'theory of marginality' was in fashion throughout Latin America. This theory appeared in all social studies on public housing in the early 1970s. Only in the 1960s did research on Brazilian housing receive an impetus. The first object of concern was the 'favelas' of Rio de Janeiro (SAGMACS, 1960; Machado da Silva, 1967; Nunes, 1976; Perlman, 1974, 1977, 1980; Leeds & Leeds, 1978). The early and mid-1960s studies were heavily influenced by the theory of social marginality. Although initially "marginal settlements" were referred to as a physical-ecological phenomenon, their population was later identified with low-income and educational traits. Influenced by theories of marginality, the National Housing Bank (BNH) developed policies of removal for the "favelados". The aim was to integrate the slum-dwellers into middle-class life by providing housing for the low income segments of society. However, many public housing complexes have been abandoned or remodelled to attract other sectors of the population as the poor abandon the new housing because it is too expensive. Thus apartment complexes were left to higher income groups who not only can afford but are delighted with the low interest rates of the BNH. Studies carried out in Rio de Janeiro in the late 1970s (Perlman, 1976, 1980) bring foward evidence that strongly indicates that the "favelados" are not marginal but in fact integrated politically and economically into society. Perlman concludes that the use of the myths of marginality are ideo-

logical justifications to carry out upper-sector policy at the expense of
the lower sectors. Nearly all writers who theorise about the politics of
the shanty-town dwellers treat a category of people as a social class on
the basis of their residential location. The inhabitants of these shanty-
towns are assumed to be either unemployed or engaged in the low-paid
tertiary sector. This perspective fails to take into account the amount
of employment and the degree to which incomes rise during periods
of rapid industrial growth. When describing the latter as marginals it
is assumed that these dwellers constitute a separate social class. This
is questionable. Data from Brazil and Chile indicate that although
unemployment is high a substantial proportion of the shanty-towns
population is, in fact, employed in the industrial sector. It is clear that
although not everyone in the shanty-towns is an industrial worker, they
are neither all 'lumpen'. In the Third World, where social classes are
often still in the process of formation, it is not possible to take a
residential category and treat it as if one were dealing with a homo-
geneous social class. Some settlements are really working class neighborhoods. More recent studies reveal the importance of squatter settlements in other urban centers. The literature on Sao Paulo (Kowarick,
1975, 1980; Pasternak Taschner, 1978; IPT/FUPAB, 1979; Camargo et
al., 1982; E. Blay, 1978; J. Wilheim, 1982) suggests that the Paulista
"favelas" are of more recent creation than their counterparts in Rio de
Janeiro and that their growth rate is accelerating.

   The literature written on governmental housing policy tends to concentrate on the period beginning with the creation of the BNH in 1964.
For housing policy prior to the BNH, Bondukie (1982) presents a
systematic survey of both the public and private sectors of the housing
market in Sao Paulo. The predominance of rented housing is explained
by analysing the structural characteristics of the Paulista economy.
Bondukie's various studies concentrating on the period between 1880
and 1920 are a basic source for anyone interested in the history of the
housing issue in Brazil. Bondukie's work concentrates on the "structural
constraints" in explaining the provision of housing by the coffee industry
in Sao Paulo. But the latter does not account properly as to how
interests were articulated and aggregated nor does he provide a political
analysis explaining why the majority of the population relied on rented
accommodation. Other studies that deal with the pre-BNH policies
concentrate on the 1930–64 period. Azevedo (1979; 1982) analyses the
early attempts of public housing institutions. He suggests that the
"Foundation for Popular Housing" followed policies of clientelism and
populism which were prevalent at the time. Azevedo's analysis of the
latter institution sees the central government as "controlling" housing
policy. This approach fails to analyse public housing policy by looking

at the "from below" logic and thus fails to grasp that state policies are a result of compromises between private and public interests and between local and regional groups.

Many studies were also interested in the aspects closely tied to the creation of the BNH analysing the new political and economic model (Azevedo, 1975; Bolaffi 1976 and 1977; Batley, 1979). The core argument of all these studies was that the crisis of the housing market was influenced not only by inflation but by the various rent laws. Sociologists such as Bolaffi explain the creation of the BNH as a response of the military regime to potential conflicts which could arise from the "favelas". Others (Souza, 1974; Andrade, 1976) analysed the new government's promotion of civil construction as a way to both reduce unemployment and create political stability. While trying to explain the background to the foundation of the BNH, the various public and social administration approaches are insistent in their refrain that power lies where it is supposed to lie, formally or legally (Azevedo, 1975; Brandao, 1983). No attention is given to channels of influence on or within political institutions; informal influence is seen as not quite legitimate. This typically excludes reference to the political ambitions and characteristics of individuals in formally important positions (e.g., Castello Branco; Sandra Cavalcanti; Roberto Campos and Carlos Lacerda. See Chapter 2). Although these studies draw attention to a broader social role of the state in maintaining the legitimacy, particularly in attempting to offset social conflicts threatening the political stability of the social system, they are confined to the analysis of low income sectors of the population. There is no mention of either the military regime's trying to co-opt the urban sectors or of the latter's influence on state housing policies. Other recent studies place much emphasis on low-income, self-help housing programs and on issues of land rent and urban land uses. Studies of self-help housing programs were influenced by research carried out in Lima by Mangin and Turner (Mangin, 1967; Mangin and Turner, 1968). Influenced by the latter, it was argued that squatter settlements offer the urban poor a means for upward socio-economic mobility. Against this background various Brazilian researchers consider this practice as one of the main aspects of the reproduction of the labor force (Rolnik & Bondukie, 1979; Maricato, 1979). But these researchers fail to explain why the state has sometimes demolished "favelas" and engaged in urban renewal programs if these spontaneous settlements were so useful to the middle and upper sectors of society.

Authors writing from a social administration perspective (Batley, 1977, 1978, 1981, 1982) have been concerned primarily with the housing of low and moderate income families. Batley in his analysis of urban policy in the city of Sao Paulo attempts to show how organizational procedures influence social relations and are derived from interests expressed as the limits within which the organisation (e.g. BNH; CO-HAB) must operate. Briefly stated, Batley analysed the Brazilian Housing System by studying how organisational procedures exclude and include subjects. He traced the origins of those procedures by exploring the context in economic change and by examining the structure and procedures of operations of particular policies. Yet Batley's tendency to focus on bureaucratically defined issues within administrative areas has also led to a tendency to re-emphasize the urban managerialist assumption of a state apparatus which is relatively autonomous from social, class and political processes. There is a failure to connect the local data (see Batley, 1983) with any broader picture. Broader structural constraints and political determinants of the local or regional context are lost from sight thus generating misleading conclusions.

If much has been written, there are still important fields and issues that remain to be studied in depth. There are, for example, no studies linking national, state, and local politics with public housing policy between 1964 and 1985. Although other works, which analysed Brazilian society during this era, introduced the idea of a situation in which government places itself above political society and considers itself free of partisan ties (see Schmitter, 1973; O'Donnell, 1978; Batley, 1983) they fail to realize that different modes of political organizations—clientelist, corporatist and autonomous—can co-exist. O'Donnell's 'bureaucratic-authoritarianism' clearly overlaps with many aspects of what Schmitter calls "state corporatism". According to this literature, the new military regime in Brazil (since 1964) has sought to replace the democratic government with authoritarian rule supposedly legitimated by a restored sense of political and social order and by a renewal of economic growth. Successful economic "development", in turn, is expected to create the necessary popular support among a minority for the restructuring of the political system, eventually allowing for reduced levels of repression as the new regime gains hegemonic control. The opposition that will emerge will be highly restricted and will in no sense challenge the regime.

The following are the principal characteristics of a "bureaucratic authoritarian" type of state:

1. Its social base is drawn from the upper fractions of a highly oligopolised and transnationalised bourgeoisie.
2. Its institutions comprise organisations in which specialists in coercion as well as those whose aim it is to achieve 'normalisation' of the economy have a decisive weight.

3. It endeavours to depoliticise social issues by dealing with them in terms of the supposedly neutral and objective criteria of technical rationality.
4. It excludes the previously active popular sectors from both political and economic participation.
5. It suppresses the institutions of popular democracy, and closes democratic channels of access to government.[4]

The main argument developed throughout this book is that taken the case of social policy, the claims (accepted at face value) that in Brazil there exists a consistent commitment to rational, bureaucratic or tecnocratic norms of government is questionable. The adequacy of the "bureaucratic authoritarian" concept in its application to Brazil is examined throughout the book.

From Neo-Marxism to Patronage-Clientelism

The history of social policy studies in non-democratic regimes has been the history of the development of alternative theoretical frameworks vying together for dominance. All of them have developed concepts of an analytical and critical character providing tools for the study and definition of social problems and a critical framework for dealing with alternative treatment of these issues. It is possible to observe the decisive influence of theoretical trends in the 1970s sociological thinking about social policy studies in non-democratic regimes. Most of the authors were influenced by the 'new' European urban sociology, with a clear Marxist tendency. Among those working within the theory of accumulation, Castells and Lojkine, have been feeding the debate in non-democratic nations on the relationship between the state, capitalist urbanization, housing and the conditions of reproduction of the labor force.[5]

Although no previous studies on social policies have been influenced by patronage-clientelism approaches, a growing literature suggests that important features of political systems in non-democratic regimes can be thus explained. This chapter will examine the above theories and conclude that although all have partial validity, elements from the Neo-Marxist and Patronage-clientelism theories can best explain social policies in non-democratic regimes. The purpose of this chapter is to provide an overview of current and past preoccupations of research into social policy and to contribute empirical evidence which will both refute and strengthen the various theoretical approaches.

Neo-Marxism

A starting point for neo-Marxist theories has been a recognition of the inadequacy of traditional or classical Marxist approaches to the theory of the state. In recent years Marxist urban research in Latin America has been dominated by the theoretical contributions of the French school of urban sociology. According to this approach, the central element in the analysis of the urban question is the study of urban politics, which Castells has defined as:

> The study of the specific articulation of the processes designated as 'urban' with the field of class struggle and consequently with the intervention of the political instance.[6]

In the structuralist reading of Marx the elements of this urban system are identified as:

1. P (Production)—spatial dimensions of the productions of goods, services and information.
2. C (Consumption)—spatial dimensions of the individual/collective social appropiation of the product; housing; cultural and recreational facilities.
3. E (Exchange)—spatial dimensions of the exchange between P and C, within P and within C (e.g., transport, commerce).
4. M (Management)—process of control of relationships between P, C and E (e.g., urban planning agencies, municipal institutions, etc.).

It is specifically through the management element that the urban system is articulated with the political system and the relationships between the various elements regulated.[7] This management element involving the intervention of the state and the politicization of urban demands has a critical role to play in the central issue in the urban question—the organization of the means of collective consumption.

All social classes demand access to and improvement of the collective material conditions of daily life and to resolve the contradictions that these conflicting demands create, the state increasingly intervenes in the urban process. Although state intervention in this area has specific economic functions, it is neither a spontaneous mechanism triggered by the mode of production nor exclusively the effect of action by the dominant classes—it also has a political logic with specific political effects. However, the state is also an expression and instrument of class relations, and as such it acts according to the relations of power between social classes and generally in favour of the hegemonic fraction of the dominant classes. On the other hand, this intervention is also accompanied by the political mobilization of the dominated social classes in relation to the means of collective consumption and the state apparatuses entrusted with their provision. This means the effective politicization of the urban question where demands for the means of collective consumption became treated in political terms and are strongly linked to questions of power. Thus, Castells argues that state intervention politicizes the totality of urban contradictions, transforms the state into a manager of the means of daily life and globalizes and politicizes the conflicts which emerge in this sphere.[8] He also argues that technical and social change is leading to an increase in state and political interventions which become not only the centre but the driving force of a social formation whose complexity requires centralized decision-making and control of processes.

Bureaucracy and Bureaucratism

According to Poulantzas, bureaucratism is regarded as one of the fundamental features of the capitalist type of state. He wrote that the bureaucracy itself accurately reflects the political power of the dominant classes and represents their interests in the particular economic, political and ideological conditions of the class struggle.[9] Furthermore, Poulantzas makes it clear that the motives and values of decision-makers are irrelevant to an understanding of state policies and interventions. In other words, the actions of politicians and administrators are simply the surface manifestation of underlying structural relationships, and the question of who occupies the various positions in the state apparatus, and what of their background, values and aims may be, is therefore of little significance. The claim made by Marxists that local government lacks any real autonomy and is simply the 'field agent' of the central state is a too simple characterisation as considerable variations can exist in the styles of local government. Not all of them can be dismissed in this way. Although it is hard to deny that the trend has been towards ever greater subordination of local government institutions in Brazil (i.e., COHAB/SP) to the federal government and to the major bureaucracies (e.g., the BNH) there are circumstances under which the power of local bureaucrats is dominant. Local bureaucrats, particularly those at the top of specialized departments such as planning, architecture, and public housing are professionals with expertise and allegiance to professional associations and the urban middle sectors. Their esoteric knowledge justifies their authority. Loyalty to professional associations with practical and ethical standards encourage many to claim a degree of autonomy from the demands of their political masters and also from other groups of bureaucrats. Evidence for administrative domination based on and justified by expertise is widespread in 'Paulista' public housing agencies. In some circumstances, the officials go over the heads of the politicians and bargain directly with pressure groups (e.g., construction firms) and other bureaucracies and local interests, undermining the authority of politicians.

The significance of professionalism influencing public policy has never been analysed in Brazil. Neo-Marxist approaches argue for the study of the integration of the city into broader national social processes and the low autonomy of local institutions and organizations. Evidence brought forward by the study of the production of a housing estate in Sao Paulo (see Ch. 3 & 4) is thus almost unique in showing how a public policy decision (the construction of low income housing) was altered dramatically as the result of decisions by bureaucrats, architects and construction firms in direct control of the designs.

In Castells' writings, access to public housing is limited by a whole series of criteria of selection (ability to pay regularly, size of family, etc.) which are also calculated in the private market even if they are put quantitatively at a lower level. The sources of inequality based on income, employment, and education are thus reinforced once more in public housing. Because of differential ability to gain access to the market, inequality in housing is thus reinforced by the inequality which results from the differential treatment of each class and social level by economic, institutional and cultural mechanisms of production and administration in public housing.[10] This approach does not recognize that access to public resources is a policy theme that must itself be institutional and political in character.

A broader view of the "Paulista" housing market must accept that the results of institutional access are not simply structured by the determinants of inequality in the wider society, but are either 'unintended consequences' or, alternatively and more powerfully, a consequence of the characteristics of bureaucracy and the institutional process itself. The bureaucrats themselves are often culturally interlinked with the wealthier urban sectors. Moreover, the rules may be biased not only by the intervention of political groups but by bureaucrats who perceive the rule book as a bureaucratic weapon (see ch. 4 and 5). It would be misleading to reduce this to a view of 'bureaucrats' as a relatively unified social category whose interests (for example over corruption) can be explained in isolation from the institutions in which they work and from the wider social order in which different categories of state functionaries are differently located. The easy and non-explanatory criticism of 'bureaucrats' is less important than an analysis of the process of allocation itself and of the inherent tendencies of institutional processes.

Marxist welfare analysis remains ambivalent in respect of the professional and social service bureaucracies. Thus Gough recognizes that the growth of the social sevices has created a new and powerful force with a vested interest in the future development of welfare services. What is not clear is whether the attempt on the part of these vested interests, especially professionals and civil servants, to negotiate generous salaries, pension arrangements, better service conditions, and the like, thus swelling the social budget and establishing professional dominance more firmly, is welcome to the Marxists. Perhaps Gough is alone among Marxist writers on the welfare state to recognize that professionalism is a 'double-edged sword'. But on the whole he takes a charitable view of the professions (e.g., social workers, planners) arguing that their autonomy and control over work is threatened by the demands of the capitalist state for greater managerial control and accountability. What is missing in the Marxist account is any perception of the conflict between professional power and privilege on the one hand, and the public interest on the other. Overall the relationship of state employment to the question of social welfare and the current capitalist crisis remains somewhat unclarified in Marxist literature.

The Neo-Marxist Approaches
and the Concept of Housing

Dunleavy concludes that Marxism's stress on the political influence of capital, even where the area of social life controlled by the state rather than by private firms has increased, is well born out by the importance of contractual interests' influence on housing construction policy, particularly by their exploitation of their favorable position vis-a-vis local authorities and design professions.[11] The urban public services account for a high proportion of all new construction orders and this proportion was especially high in GSP in the late 1970s and early 1980s—a period of saturation in the private housing market. Although at first the balance of market power was in the hands of local authorities the large construction firms succeeded in influencing the latter. Essentially, in seeking to insulate themselves from competition by smaller firms, the large corporations participating in the construction of the Itaquera project exerted pressure to increase the unit size and to shift to (technological) sophisticated methods of construction (see ch. 4). As most of the planning and architectural work of the Itaquera housing estate was carried out by private consultants it is not suprising that construction technology and ideology are not only dominated by the private firms but influence state agencies. In such circumstances the private sector is likely to have extensive and important influence on public policy making.

While Dunleavy, in his research on mass housing in Britain, concludes that elements of neo-Marxist analyses stressing the political power of private capital[12] were found to be considerably accurate and relevant, Rod Burgess objects to this neo-Marxist approach. He remarks that it is by no means certain that the influence of property capital on the evolution of the urban residential structures in Latin America dependent on social formations, is of the same order as that experienced in the cities of advanced capitalist societies, although there can be no doubting its presence.[13]

It is possible to analyse the influence of private capital on the 'Paulista' housing market by looking at the construction cycle. During periods of high demand large private construction firms invest in expensive housing as the profit margins in the private sector are larger and uncontrolled. During slumps the depressed market will result in either the transfer of property capital to foreign markets (a trend that exists in Brazil) or the construction of relatively inexpensive housing for the state sector. The large numbers of units constructed together with the employment of new capital intensive technologies and in some instances corrupt measures, compensate for the "controlled" low profit margins typical of the public sector.

Some Possible Implications for Marxist Approaches

The first key finding of our book is the enormous increase in the construction of public housing since 1964. Some Marxist theories of the state suggest that the actions of the state (e.g., expenditure on public housing) depend on the wider needs of capital and vary with the phases of the accumulation cycle.[14] From the perspective of Marxist political economy, patterns of a quantum increase in public housing (from 17,000 units during the period 1900–1964 to more than a million during the two decades of military regime) can be explained in the following way. Owner-occupation is seen as an important means whereby capitalists, aided and abetted by the state, have divided the working class and strengthened their control. Owner-occupiers are led to believe that ownership of a small house gives them a vested interest in the capitalist system of private property. They are, furthermore, constrained to follow a pattern of life which renders them passive workers and ideal consumers. To gain access to the owner-occupied sector they are obliged to secure steady employment and to suscribe to bourgeois values of privatism and thrift. The ties imposed by the need to make regular mortgage repayments acts as a mechanism of social control.

The military regime's commitment to owner-occupation can be explained on ideological and political grounds. Owner-occupation can be seen as fundamentally important both in fragmenting 'power blocs' and in giving the worker a stake in the system. The massive influx of rural migrants to the urban centres in the South East of Brazil during the 1970s increased dramatically the number of shantytowns and slums. The provision of state-subsidized housing makes it possible for low income groups to live in better (and otherwise unaffordable) accommodation. The continuous expansion of state investment in housing, is due indirectly to the fact that the viability of the capitalist growth depends upon ever larger investment projects and a continuous rise in the costs of providing "social overheads" such as housing. In order to encourage private capital investment, welfare states must "socialize" these continuously increasing costs and outlays. Thus, a majority of the BNH resources were invested in the heavily industrialized South East region of Brazil. Given the conditions and requirements of urbanization, large-scale concentration of labor power in industry, rapid economic and regional change, the reduced ability of the family to cope with the difficulties of life in industrial society—all of which are well-known characteristics of capitalist structures—the absence of large-scale state-subsidized housing would leave the system in a state of exploding conflict and anarchy.

Another possible explanation is provided by Poulantzas in his book 'The Crisis of the Dictatorship'. He defines two types of bourgeoisies that can be found in a military regime. The first type is called domestic bourgeoisie who is concentrated chiefly in the industrial sector. It is interested in an industrial development less polarized towards the exploitation of the country by foreign capital and in a state intervention which would guarantee it its protected markets at home, while also making it more competitive vis-a-vis foreign capital. These bourgeoisies are not simply confined to the industrial domain but also extended to fields directly dependent on the industrialization process and even services of various types. The second type, the so called "comprador bourgeoisie", can be defined as that fraction whose interests are entirely subordinated to those of foreign capital and which functions as a kind of staging-post and direct intermediary from the implementation and reproduction of foreign capital. The domestic bourgeoisie seeks an extension and development of the home market. The development of this domestic bourgeoisie coincides with the induced reproduction of the dominant relations of production within the various social formations. The distinction between "comprador" and domestic bourgeoisie is not a statistical and empirical distinction fixed rigidly once and for all. The concrete configuration depends to a certain extent on the conjuncture.

Poulantzas in his book deals with three dictatorships: Greece, Portugal and Spain. Although Poulantzas does not deal directly with Latin America, several aspects of his analysis are of important relevance to a study of Brazilian politics. He states that it is wrong to see these bourgeoisies as constantly and systematically bullied by the military. Besides the advantages that these bourgeoisies themselves drew from the "domestic peace" the (military) regimes often promoted and sometimes even sought their development.[15] In both the Greek and Brazilian case the bourgeoisie had itself clearly supported the actual establishment of the military dictatorship in the face of the rise of popular struggles. The development of the domestic bourgeoisie under these military regimes increased their demand for a growing share of state support, e.g., that the state should take more account of its own particularistic interests. Poulantzas suggests that the structural organisation of the state apparatus is sufficient to ensure that it acts on behalf of the middle sectors.

In answering the question why the state serves the interests of the bourgeoisie (e.g., expenditure on housing programs) Poulantzas states that it does so because of its structure. Whatever the social background of the occupants of the state apparatus, they cannot alter the nature of the state. What the neo-Marxist approaches in general (and Poulantzas' approach in particular) do not explain is why should a military regime allocate a large proportion of public expenditure on social services to a sector of the population that not only supports them but helped bring them to power?

An assertion by Marxist writers that governments serve the interests of capitalism can be made an empirical propositon if evidence shows that it is false wholly or partly and that it is truer of some periods and of some nations than of others. On the evidence available, my opinion is that the interests of capitalism are one important element in social policy in non-democratic regimes. As we have seen, neo-Marxist theories on their own do not adequately explain state reaction to social policy in non-democratic regimes. Such analyses may provide a starting point for discussion but are, in themselves, inadequate. The patronage clientelism approach explains an aspect neglected by the neo-Marxists, that is, what kinds of influences the urban sectors have on the distribution of social services. Rather we suggest that a satisfactory theoretical explanation must embrace elements from the patronage-clientelism and the neo-Marxist school of thought.

Patronage-Clientelism Approach

Definitions

One school of thought has identified machine politics or patron-clientelism as the dominant feature of the organization of mass support for political parties in the Third World.[16] The core of this system of machine politics is the exchange of economic and social favors to a poor and socially fragmented population in return for party support. Parallels are drawn between machine politics in Third World party systems and similar phenomena in United States urban party politics (especially New York and Chicago) in the late nineteenth century. Machine politics integrate a diverse network of class and ethnic interests into a loose coalition of allies seeking to control the state and convert it into a source of patronage and material rewards for individuals.

There are, unfortunately, almost as many definitions of the patron-client relationship as there are writers on the subject. I will use a synthesis of various definitions. The former relationship is defined as:

> a special type of dyadic exchange, distinguishable by the following characteristics:
>
> (a) the relationship between actors of unequal power and status;
> (b) the principle of reciprocity; that is, a self-regulating form of interpersonal exchange, the maintenance of which depends on the return that each actor expects to obtain by rendering goods and services to the other and which ceases once the expected rewards fail to materialize;
> (c) a particularistic and private relationship, anchored only loosely in public law or community norms.[17]

More loosely defined observations about clientelism can be found in the vast literature on Latin American politics: concepts such as landlord–peasant relationships, of caudillos, personalism, and in analyses of "corruption" in bureaucracies, business firms and political organizations.[18] In the more recent literature, the patron-client exchange becomes central to an understanding of how some political systems work, constituting in some instances the most important basis of interest articulation and socio-political control.

Patronage-Clientelism Systems

Unlike feudalism (a method of government in which the essential relationship is between lord and vassal), patrimonialism as a political system operates through a specialized administrative officialdom appointed by and responsible to the ruler.[19] It is possible to differentiate between two forms of patrimonialism. In the traditional form, the relationship between patrons and clients has penetrated the entire political entity. The relationship between ruler and subject is one of reciprocal loyalties based on expectations of mutual benefit. The maintenance of a clientelistic nature of individual relations at the local level of government structures is due to the fact that the political system has a limited distributive capacity and resources are distributed for purposes of political recruitment. The period of the First Republic (1889–1930) was one in which "coronelismo"—a term used as a designation of the locally powerful-dominated state and federal politics in Brazil. The political dominance of the landowners gave rise to a pattern of unconditional support for the local boss and for the official state party.

> The pattern of local factionalism and consistent support for the state party is best understood in terms of commitment to the interests represented and policies pursued at regional and federal level, and to a strong state party as a guarantee of effective action in national politics.[20]

In modernizing patrimonialism, the second form of patrimonialism, transactions originate from traditional sectors and from the party, bureaucracy and trade unions. Government officials, businessmen and the new "professionals" are all part of the diversified forms of patronage. Under those new circumstances, elections became devices through which the 'clientele' register loyalty to competing patrons through the voting system. Modern patrimonial systems developed not only a vast variety of clientage networks but also diversified their networks (e.g., by the incorporation of the urban middle sectors in the course of the post-1964 military regime in Brazil).

From the 1930s it is possible to find signs of "modernizing patrimonialism" in Brazil. The expansion of the state bureaucracy during the Vargas regime and its irreversible acquisition of new functions gave the final blow to the 'traditional' type of patronage where coronelismo monopolised all mediations between society and the political elite. The Vargas regime expanded state intervention to protect and encourage the growth of different sectors through the creation of "autarquias". During the 1950s, 1960s and 1970s state expansion in Brazil's economy occurred not only through the growth of its activities but also through the creation of new areas of government action (e.g., the creation of the BNH in 1965). Under Vargas after 1930, with authority and control concentrated in the presidency, the federal bureaucracy's growth and influence expanded rapidly. The creation of the Administrative Department of the Public Service (DASP) in 1938 did not succeed in sheltering the bureaucracy from the sway of patronage. Although the Brazilian law stated that the recruitment of public employees should follow merit standards (as of 1945), political patronage remained the main criteria.

The rise of the urban sector and the decline of the old landowner leadership resulted from the Vargas period onwards. Getulio sought independence from the regional elites and succeeded in mobilizing the urban population. The autonomy of the regions was not only being throttled by the expansion of the state administration, but also by the increasing power of those who controlled the party machinery at the national level. These changes indicate a clear shift from "oligarchic" to "bureaucratic, party oriented" patronage which we can identify while analysing the evolution of public housing policy during the mid-1940s and the 1950s. Not suprisingly, to preserve their economic and political hegemony, dominant interests preferred the new urban sector to enter the Brazilian political system not as autonomous actors but more typically as dependent subjects of a paternalistic order. One of the prime examples of this new strategy was the creation of a national housing agency—the Foundation for Popular Housing. Political considerations were seen as heavily influencing the decision to create this new housing institution and its distribution policy. As demand outpaced supply, clientelism, at sectorial and regional levels, became a characteristic of the state housing market. A significant proportion of the agency's resources were allocated to a fairly new and rapidly expanding sector of the urban sector—public servants. At the spatial level of analysis, the distribution of housing by states and regions is noted by the heavy bias to the South East where most of the urban sector is concentrated. The lack of housing in the North East and the South, is explained as a result of a low level of political expression. These trends were incremented in later years (see chapter 4) especially under the military regime.

Patron-Client Relations
in Pre–Twentieth Century Brazil

Before examining patron-client relationships it is worth noticing how very little has been written on the subject. One of the earliest studies was on rural clientelism published in 1948.[21] Leal influenced later works on rural clientele in the various regions of Brazil. In recent years a few studies have pointed out that the concept of "patron-dependent" or "patron-client" relations offers a fruitful approach to the understanding of certain significant and widespread patterns of political behaviour in Brazil.[22] Brazilian society in colonial times has to be seen primarily in terms of a fairly large number of units—mainly agricultural plantations. The relationship between landowners and peasants was similar to that of feudalism in medieval Europe. Politics was an extension of private life. The plantation owners "ruled" not only over their family but also their dependents and slaves, and protected them from the interference of outsiders. At the macro-level of analysis, the colonial government was a 'patrimonial system' with the king claiming full personal power. The royal administrative apparatus was composed of bureaucrats who were personally bound to the king and thus prevented the emergence of a feudal-style landed aristocracy. After independence in the 1850s new agencies with special tasks in the areas of government, politics and religion, began to replace the patriarchal family units. The urban upper sectors appeared and were used by the king to oppose the rural patriarchate. Political parties and a decentralized local government machinery were set up in a very limited way (only one percent of the population was allowed to vote), to channel public opinion.

From the start of this era, political parties were vehicles for the expression of the personal power and the fulfillment of the personal ambitions of the heads of the patriarchal clans. They were never anything other than convenient receptacles for the captive votes of the dependents of the local powerful. These parties gave Brazil an intensely personalist political system, which it retained throughout its modern history.[23] The new bureaucrats or political leaders not only expected but rewarded personal loyalty and used their positions to further their interests. In rural society, peasants were expected to support the patron in his quest for political office or to elect the patron's candidates. This latter relation is referred to as coronelismo. The coronel who is a kind of local super-patron not only secures the election of loyal lieutenants to local political positions, but delivers the votes of his dependents upwards. He contributes to the state and federal elections and rewards his dependents with jobs in the bureaucracy.

Recent Changes in Urban Politics

While in some areas things have hardly changed, in others political patronage relationships have been modified especially since the mid-1940s. Urban politics, trade unionism and the civil service became new spheres of traditional patron-dependency relationships. Even in the rural areas of Brazil, peasants have learned that votes are a valuable merchandise and they demand a price for their vote. The personal nature of the relationship between political patron and client has changed into a situation where politicians secure votes not only by providing a job but also by presenting 'platforms' which are concerned with promises of providing 'goods' not at an individual level but at a community level (e.g., promises of electricity and housing). Politicians, like Maluf the state governor of Sao Paulo, amassed large followings by demagoguery and emphasizing distinct issues or concrete social programs.

Vague promises of housing reforms appealed to the urban middle sectors who were frustrated as they perceived that although a few can reach a certain degree of affluence and gain political power, the sector as a whole, because of the steady deterioration of the Brazilian economy, had been incapable of keeping up with the economic demands of modern life. Escalating prices and diminishing buying power in the recent past resulted in the members of the middle sectors being affected most and paying the highest tolls in the Brazilian drive for modernization. Members of the middle sectors experienced the declining power of their salaries and an increase in the gap between their expectations (to own cars and houses) and their economic capabilities.

Confronted with this, the reaction of PDS politicians was to attract newly emerging urban constituencies by appealing to their inarticulate discontent and economic frustrations. These strategies produced the electoral majorities needed to launch politicians (e.g., Paulo Maluf) and sustain them in power. Election campaigns, at municipal, state, and federal levels, have in recent years supplied evidence of politicians securing votes by such procedures as promising the provision of public housing to certain communities. At the state level, Paulo Maluf presented non-ideological platforms in his electoral campaign for governorship of Sao Paulo and at the federal level the Minister of Interior, Mario Andreazza, promised the "Nordestinos" public investments in urban infrastructure.

Previously, casting a vote for the patron's candidate was the unquestioned means by which the client fulfilled his side of the bargain. In the present context, urban masses use their vote to strengthen their bargaining position. Candidates who can deliver public goods before the elections, rather than promise them for after the elections, have advantage over their opponents. Politicians, such as state governors and federal ministers, who control the allocation of public resources (e.g., public housing) have a huge advantage over opposition candidates.[24]

In a system like this election is obviously neither the results of ideological commitments, nor of the class interests of the electorate. It is a system which has contributed greatly to party political weakness in Brazil. Party support is on the whole irrelevant to the creation of an electoral base.

On the contrary: parties exist by virtue of the votes which politicians are willing to bring to them.[25]

Viewed from this perspective, there are a number of reasons why the literature on clientelism should commend itself to the attention of researchers interested in non-democratic regimes. Basically the concept of clientelism reconciles otherwise contradictory perceptions of domestic power relationships within non-democratic regimes themselves. One example is the apparent contrast between references to the existence of Latin American ruling elites and approaches emphasizing the fragmentation of power into the hands of many competing "power contenders". While the patron-client exchange is based on hierarchical distributions of resources and power, the concept simultaneously allows for the possibility of intense conflict between narrowly based, shifting patron-client clusters and pyramids. It is not suprising that although patron-client relationships exist not only in underdeveloped areas such as Latin America they thrive in unevenly developed economies. In non-democratic economies, access to public resources is not determined by Weberian notions of bureaucratic procedures.

To a much greater extent than in developed economies, individuals neither gain access as of right to these services nor are they are debarred from access by standardized qualifications. Under these conditions, vertical relationships of the patron-client type are convenient means to increase state control over local areas.[26]

In authoritarian regimes the military is concerned with potential threats to political order. By creating a network of patron-client relationships between state agencies and the urban sector and by providing welfare services, the state becomes the major source of survival of the latter.

Structure of the Book

Against this background I will provide an empirically-based analysis of public housing policies in Greater Sao Paulo from 1964 up to 1986. The period analysed covers nearly two decades of military rule. Although it was only in January 1985 that Presidential elections were held and the military returned to the barracks, the results of the elections of November 1982 made irreversible the trend towards "abertura". A genuine case of "decompression from above", the elections involved all the members of the federal and state assemblies, the municipalities, one third of the Senate and, most important, for the first time since 1965, the state governments. Only the Presidential elections remained to be elected indirectly by an electoral college. Sao Paulo was chosen principally because it represents the most economically and politically important state in Brazil and because it received a disproportionately large percentage of the National Housing Bank's resources.

The main argument to be presented here attempts to cover two crucial areas which at present have not been explored in non-democratic regimes. Firstly, the thesis addresses the topic of the attitudes of the military government to public housing policy. Secondly, it enquires into the political dimension of public housing policy at national, regional, state and local levels. In searching for the relationship between the government and the public housing issue the work will analyse with empirical evidence why in a bureaucratic authoritarian state did the political aspect have such an important influence on the allocative process of public housing. Drawing on empirical evidence, we can suggest five reasons for this milieu in Brazil.

1. Although military regimes do not depend on popular legitimacy to survive, they do need the cooperation of the urban sectors who keep society operating from day to day. Usually, the dread by the latter of economic crisis and civil unrest causes these groups to accept military rule in times of crisis. Once order is restored and economic conditions improve, they are among the first to demand that the armed forces step aside so that civilian politicians can return to their offices. In the congressional elections of November 1974, the urban sectors voted decisively against the government as their economic conditions had gained from the so-called "Brazilian miracle", although the military's intentions during this period of rapid economic growth had been to increase the government's popularity. The subsequent decade has been a period in which the government tried to increase the support of the urban sector by political juggling. While congressional and gubernatorial elections have been opened up, the military was able to keep ultimate political control by allocating public housing to the large urban centers (especially during election campaigns); by buying votes (e.g., in the Northeast states); by increasing the bureaucratic intimidation and delay and the political manipulations of rules in public housing agencies; by queuing for housing which, used as an administrative response to scarcity of resources, became a political manipulative tool; and by an increase of corruptive measures (especially during the Maluf period).

2. Most of the literature on the Brazilian political system has underestimated the capacity of the urban population to appropriate more than their fair share of public expenditure. They demand more resources for better housing in their areas; they complain vociferously if they have to wait too long; they demand that the state intervene to subsidise

their mortgages. Too often these pressures have been successful, and in consequence the distribution of public spending has been tilted away from the areas of greatest need to those which generate the loudest and best organised demands. The elaborate rules of the housing institutions have not only been biased by the intervention of the urban sector but are linked with the cultural attitudes of the bureaucrats themselves.

3. The willingness of the federal government to implement "pharaonic" projects such as the TransAmazonica, Itaipu and the construction of a massive amount of low quality housing projects (e.g., in the North East—see ch. 2) was a cheap way of simulating a concern with poverty, a token, a symbolic gesture and little more. Such pharaonic projects were used by the military regime to buy-off discontent. It also served as an instrument of political quiescence and symbolic reassurance, thereby immobilizing potentially troublesome individuals and groups. The successful tokenistic nature of "pharaonic" projects (quite a few financed by the BNH—see ch. 2) masked the real political, social, and economic issues by demonstrating what a successful job was being done by the government.

4. The rapid growth of the public sector in Brazil has had an enormous effect on political and economic development. Although bureaucrats are supposed to be the servants of political officials, the latter often find themselves the captives of their bureaucrats. They rely on them when they design policies as well as when they implement them. The construction of large and expensive public housing complexes (see Ch. 3) expresses not only the wish of architects to experiment with new housing styles but also the government's desire to reward the technocracy. Housing projects in the large urban centers (mainly in Rio de Janeiro, Greater Sao Paulo and Brasilia) have been constructed to accommodate technocratic groups such as the military, bank employees and key civil servants (e.g., in Brasilia).

Public housing agencies have frequently promoted themselves as having an "agency ideology" concerning policy. Forced to operate within certain income parameters which still present overwhelming demand, institutions such as COHAB have resorted to the application of procedures which select low risk candidates thus restricting demand. By disguising exclusion and creating diversionary queues COHAB has succeeded in permitting the allocation of housing to selected groups (see ch. 3 & 4). Our study supports the view that the Brazilian bureaucracy supports only changes that secure and assure its political hegemony; once in power the bureaucracy is unwilling to share economic rewards or political power with the popular sector.[27]

5. Violation of administrative rules and procedures by government officials constitutes a major obstacle to the effective implementation of

national housing programs. Whatever positive functions bureaucratic corruption may have in bending inappropriate or excessively rigid regulations or directives, the realization of central planning goals can be impeded to the extent that individual functionaries can change or negotiate their assigned tasks. Official corruption,and the imperfect hierarchical control that it indicates, occurs in all Paulista public housing agencies (see chapter 3).

Throughout the book, I argue that the increase of public expenditure on social services in Brazil is a result of technocratic necessity, political clientelism and of a quest to remove political pressures. We must now ask if, in some respects, this situation is special to Brazil or does it also prevail in other non-democratic regimes (e.g., in Asia). The authoritarian government in Brazil intensified the process of providing social services as a 'solution' to the problems of uneven income distribution and to the lack of secure internal bases of support for their regime. Like most other non-democratic regimes, Brazil showed no interest in social policies in the pre-World War II period, but the relentless growth of the national populations and the tendency for people to concentrate in ever larger cities has generated more concern. The rapid growth of the urban population led to the concentration of large groups of low income households in a few large cities. This in turn complicated the task of providing social services.

In practically all non-democratic regimes the role of the state is dominant in all areas of social, economic and political activities. The governments of middle-income, medium sized economies have an inevitable influence over the distribution of welfare services as central government has a strong control over local expenditures. The highly centralized authoritarian regimes deny official parties a substantial role in government. Rather, they create powerful political-machines, built on resources controlled by the state, which organise electoral support to sustain programs with only minority appeal. In advanced industrializing nations where the system can be labelled closed (where the state apparatus itself monopolizes economic and social power) social policies generally respond to the institutional interests of the groups that dominate the government machinery. Interestingly, although a unified core may dominate organized political activity in the country, such a system may not have sufficient power to force compliance from the middle and low income sectors. In this case, privileged groups in the "modern" sector of these countries generate demands with which the government must comply to forestall violence or public dissent.

In attempting to relate our findings to "development theory" it is important to define the latter:

Poor countries have special characteristics that tend to create a different role for the government. These characteristics and this expanded or emphasized role for government, particularly as it affects economic growth, tend to make the operations of the public adminstrator significantly different. Where such differences exist, public administration can be usefully called development administration.[28]

Development theorists identify some of the more common features of the politics of development. The principal ones are:

1. A high degree of reliance on the political sector for achieving results in society.
2. Widespread political instability.
3. Modernizing elitist leadership, accompanied by a wide "political gap" between the rulers and the ruled.
4. An imbalance in the growth of political institutions, with the bureaucracy among those in the more mature category.[29]

One of the ways that enable military regimes to remain in power is by investing in social programs. This reduces widespread political instability as technocrats, bureaucrats (and in general groups that support the government machinery) and even low income sectors are allocated social services. The distributive process of allocating public goods is not related to the question of equality but to specific concepts that are widespread in the Third World literature: co-optation, patronage, clientelism and bureaucratic "rings". "Bureaucratic rings" can be defined as clusters of particularistic interests that are bound to the state bureaucracy by clientelism and co-optation. These "rings" are neither brought together as a class nor as an elite but simply as a group that is politically competitive both with each other and with outsiders.

Most academic literature on policymaking is based on examples from advanced industrialized countries. This literature is insightful, but limited by the relationship between policymaking and other givens features of these societies. They have high levels of public information, a wide distribution of power, political parties and parliamentary systems. Much of the vocabulary used to describe or analyse these systems is not very useful for non-democratic states. Lobbying, interest articulation, judicial review, interest group politics, decentralization and legislative reform have little relationship to contemporary policymaking in non-democratic regimes, with few exceptions.

Following the introduction, Chapter 2 will describe the evolution of Brazil's social policy from 1880 to 1986 and pave the way for the later analysis of how economic and political factors influenced the governments' policies. We draw attention to the appearance of political clientelism in new forms of bureaucratic, urban and even industrial settings and its continuing role in linking investment in social policies to a dynamic of political interests. The intervention of the state from the dictatorship of Getulio Vargas onwards did not limit itself to the creation of housing saving schemes. Much more important was the recognition that through housing policies the government could win the sympathy of the popular sectors. The second section of this chapter deals with the federal housing system. The background to the foundation of the National Housing Bank in 1964 is surveyed by looking at the economic and political policies of the Castello Branco government (1964–67). During this period state involvement in the economy increased rapidly. The creation of the BNH is analysed together with the organizational structure of the BNH, and the composition of its revenues and financial costs. In a second phase the BNH in the 1970s underwent operational transformations and broadened its functions. During a period of rapid urban and industrial expansion the Bank began to give greater priority to financing projects aimed at higher income levels.

Regional and inter-regional distribution of public housing is seen as of great political significance when looking at the BNH's programs. During the 1970s nearly 60 percent of the Bank's resources had been distributed to the rich urban industrial areas of the South-East. The state and local governments in this region not only supported the military regime but were strongholds of the ruling party (PDS). Since the 1980s, when the South-East region became a stronghold of the opposition parties they lost a substantial proportion of BNH funds which were diverted to the 'pro-PDS' governments of the Northeast region. This chapter also analyses national politics, from 1964 to 1983, and shows that the politics of housing is strongly tied to the former (national politics) and even to regional politics as shown in Chapter 3 (especially during the Maluf period). The process of redemocratization and the return of the civilian government is evaluated in relation to social policy.

Chapters 3 and 4 provide empirical material to illustrate a main theme of this study. Why does Brazil, a military and non-competitive regime, have a tendency to expand its expenditure in social services such as public housing? Although at first it seems that state intervention in this area is justified in order to promote a more efficient functioning of the economy and that there are aspects of this policy which seem to be aimed at attaining a minimum standard below which no one should fall, there have been few attempts to establish whether this really is the case in the Brazilian society. Chapter 3 describes and analyses the housing market in Greater Sao Paulo by investigating three public housing agencies. The belief that public expenditure on public housing benefits the less well-off is widespread. Long waiting lists for state and municipal housing are a phenomenon which has become an instrument for the control of the urban sectors. When analysing the distributive role of COHAB, CODESPAULO and INOCOOP we can see that the allocation of state and municipal housing is channelled partly on the basis of political advantage. Through judicious use of patronage, political ties are strengthened and political support deepened. Many instances of patronage politics were evident especially during the electoral campaigns of 1974, 1978 and 1982. State governors intervened directly in the various housing programs of COHAB/SP and CODES-PAULO. Ambitious politicians, such as the Paulista state governor Paulo Maluf, promised in their electoral campigns that they would allocate resources in the direction of the construction of public housing if they would be nominated, but they defied their "platform promises" when the opposition won the local votes. High level bureaucratic jobs such as the presidency of COHAB and CODESPAULO, which were once reserved for technocrats, have been transformed into political positions. For example with the election of Maluf as state governor all the high level bureaucratic jobs at CODESPAULO were handed out as rewards to his close supporters without consideration of their technical quali-fications.

Public policies engage the power of the state to channel resources, benefits and privileges preferentially to some members of society over others. The policies sponsored by a regime can redistribute advantages among those already benefiting from the system, or extend advantage to groups that represent political threats. Another interpretation of the growth of expenditure on housing programs appears if we analyse cooperative housing agencies. INOCOOP provided housing at special financial conditions mainly to technocrats who are members of trade unions. Unlike the other two housing agencies there are no direct links with political parties, or with the election cycle, but with the Ministry of Labor (the other two agencies are influenced by the Ministry of Interior which administers the Federal Housing System). Trade union housing programs (such as PROSINDI) are one more way of limiting the unions' autonomy and controlling them even more. By investing in schemes such as cooperative housing, the government makes sure that despite the opposition parties gaining a majority in the Congressional elections, they eventually have little influence over the way the country is governed. The growth in the size and influence of technocrats can be seen as a necessary product of economic and social change. The strongest use of technocratic power is the defence of its own status and privileges. A clear example is the construction of high-rise public housing (mainly in Sao Paulo, Rio de Janeiro and Brasilia) for a clientele consisting of technocrats who have the ability to extract more benefits from the public services and absorb resources for their convenience. For the military government the construction of housing for the technocracy is of particular significance as it believes that the latter have an important role in stabilising society, in expanding the national markets and in maintaining social cohesion. It is also clear that technocratic ideologies are extremely influential in most service areas of government. The government employs increasing numbers of members of professional groups who enjoy not only a high status and prestige but also a high disproportionate percentage of public resources (e.g., public housing).

Chapter 4 analyses the most recent and influential housing development in Greater Sao Paulo-Itaquera, built by the municipal housing agency during the late 1970s. After analysing the socio-economic structure of the population who received public housing in Itaquera, by using various statistical tests to establish relations between different variables (such as: level of education; income; profession; place of origin; previous type of housing), we find evidence that the average income and level of education of the inhabitants is much higher than that of the "Paulista" population as a whole. A large proportion of the housing units in Itaquera were allocated to public sector employees and to highly skilled industrial workers while only a small number of units was constructed for the low income sectors. The low income inhabitants were mainly removed from "favelas". This forms part of a government policy, going back to 1936, to transfer the inhabitants to other areas and eradicate the "favelas" from their original location or in other instances upgrade them. The military regime's repressive attitude of removing "favelados" is a result of a policy to exclude low-income participation and suppress the demands of the urban poor. By constructing housing for the low income population military regimes seek to exclude them from political participation, thus removing a potential support for middle-sector political parties and reducing pressure to adopt welfare. Clearly, for half a century, military regimes have been perpetuating subversive policies.

Chapter 5 will explain the logic behind social policy expenditure in non-democratic regimes. It will also analyse the influence of international aid agencies in shaping patterns of public expenditure. Finally the redemocratization process in non-democratic regimes will be analysed vis-a-vis social policy.

Notes

1. P. Schmitter, "The Portugalization of Brazil", in A. Stepan, *Authoritarian Brazil* (New Haven: Yale University Press, 1973), p. 195.
2. See Gary Wynia, *The Politics of Latin American Development* (USA: Cambridge University Press, 1984); S. Hughes and K. Mijeski, *Politics of Public Policy in Latin America* (USA: Westview Press, 1984).
3. See Chapter 2.
4. G. O'Donnell, "Tensions in the Bureaucratic-Authoritarian State and the Question of Democracy" in D. Collier Ed., *The New Authoritarianism in Latin America* (USA: Princeton, 1979), pp. 292–293.
5. L. Valladares, *Housing in Brazil: An Introduction to Recent Literature* (Rio de Janeiro: IUPERJ, 1982), p. 2.
6. M. Castells, *The Urban Question* (London: Edward Arnold, 1977), p. 244.
7. *Ibid.*
8. *Ibid*, pp. 42–43.
9. N. Poulantzas, *Political Power and Social Classes* (London: New Left Books, 1973), p. 345.
10. M. Castells, *Urban.*
11. P. Dunleavy, *The Politics of Mass Housing in Britain* (Oxford: Claredon Press, 1981), p. 183.
12. *Ibid.*
13. R. Burgess, "The Politics of Urban Residence in Latin America", in *International Journal of Urban and Regional Research* (Vol. 6: 1982), p. 489.
14. See O'Connor (1973); Castells (1976).
15. N. Poulantzas, *The Crisis of the Dictatorship* (London: New Left Books, 1976), p. 47.
16. J. Scott, *Comparative Political Corruption*(New Jersey: Prentice Hall, 1972).
17. R. Kaufman, "The Patron-Client Concept and Macro-Politics", in *Comparative Studies in Society and History* (Vol. 3: June 1974), p. 285.
18. *Ibid.*
19. R. Lemarchande & K. Legg, "Political Clientelism and Development", in *Comparative Politics* (Vol. 4., No. 3: January 1972).
20. P. Cammack, "Clientelism and Military Government in Brazil", in C. Clapham *Private Patronage and Public Power* (England: Pinter, 1982), p. 56.
21. V. Leal, *O Coronelismo, Enaxada e Voto* (Rio de Janeiro: 1948).
22. See Peter Flynn, *Brazil–A Political Analysis* (England: E. Benn, 1978).
23. E. de Kadt, *Catholic Radicals in Brazil* (Oxford: Oxford University Press, 1970), p. 1.
24. See: Chapter 5.
25. de Kadt, *Ibid* p. 33.
26. Bryan Roberts, *Cities of Peasants* (England: E. Arnold, 1981), p. 156.

27. See S. Lipset and A. Solari, *Elites in Latin America* (New York: Oxford University Press, 1964).

28. I. Swerdlow (ed), *Development Administration: Concepts and Problems* (Syracuse: Syracuse University Press, 1963), p. 14.

29. H. Ferrel, *Public Administration* (USA: Prentice Hall, 1966).

2

Financing Social Policy:
The Brazilian National Housing Bank
and Its Predecessors

This chapter is an outline of the evolution of Brazil's housing policy up to 1986. I shall look at the kinds of changes that occurred since the beginning of the twentieth century and estimate the extent to which these changes shaped the pattern of change to come, particularly the creation of the BNH. While analysing the organizational structure of the BNH and the composition of its revenues and financial costs this chapter highlights the essential political nature of the planning process in Brazil, in contrast to the rational-comprehensive or 'technocratic' model which is often assumed to predominate. The selective provision of subsidized housing was used to buy urban political support and to relieve social and economic pressures. The advent of a civilian government in 1985 brought forth changes in housing policy. The major change was the dismantling of the BNH and the decentralization of housing policy.

The Private Provision of Social Welfare

Before the 1930s, most social welfare and assistance was in private hands: in the period of Portuguese colonialism, the Church or Church-related bodies, provided limited help in times of need. During the beginning of the twentieth century various private forms of social welfare continued to support the needy sectors. The generation of the First Republic (1889–1930), faced with revolutionary metropolitan demographic changes, saw the need for new municipal concepts, and for a new approach to urban planning and social control. The new urban order in Brazil, which lasted from 1889 to the 1920s, coupled with complementary policies at the national level, fostered an elitist government that cared little about the poor and downtrodden, and nearly dismantled the traditions of preceding centuries. The growth of voluntary associations, mutual aid societies, and of savings from obligatory funds, which some companies set up to provide their employees with funeral benefits, retirement payments and medical aid in return for their regular contributions. In the area of housing policy, the period between 1886 and 1918 was characterized by the presence of "corticos"—slum dwellings—as the most common solution for popular housing. Although the situation of the housing market was criticized by both the public and private sectors, rented housing and "corticos" remained the typical solution to the working classes' severe dwelling conditions.

The late nineteenth century was a period when a massive influx of immigrants disembarked in the province of Sao Paulo. The growth of the city of Sao Paulo was linked to the rate of migration. Between 1886 and 1900 the population increased dramatically—from less than fifty thousand to nearly a quarter of million inhabitants. The rapid growth of the population caused the public sector and the dominant classes to preoccupy themselves with the housing conditions of the labor force. During this period, "Villas Operarias" (complexes of houses) began to be constructed by the industries in order to to be rented at low prices or even offered free to its workers. Between 1870 and 1880, in the early phase of industrial growth, the short supply of labor was reduced due to an expansion of industry and Bahia, Rio de Janeiro, Minas Gerais and Sao Paulo became manufacturing centers. Several industrialists built "workers towns" (Villas Operarias) which were usually constructed alongside the factories and houses were either let or sold to the employees. All the "Villas" were situated outside the city of Sao Paulo and existed mainly during the second half of the nineteenth century. During that period there was a shortage of labor, a crisis initiated by the abolishment of slavery.

Although the crisis really existed in Sao Paulo it had a different solution. In the 1880s, when the industry started to expand in Sao Paulo, the bourgoisie of the coffee industry, in order to have a sufficient workforce, initiated subsidized immigration. There were not only sufficient numbers of immigrants to work in this important sector of the Paulista economy but also enough workers to create an ample industrial reserve army. Thus, if we take into consideration the absolute growth of population compared to the growth of demand for industrial work, it is possible to speak about a lack of workers.

A report by the State Department of Employment in 1919 supplies us with empirical data that puts beyond any doubt the importance, at least quantitative, of the "Villas Operarias" constructed by the industry in Sao Paulo city (only a very low percentage provided housing to their labor force). Bondukie concludes that mostly these "villas operarias" existed because of an operational necessity of industries whose sites were far or inaccessible by means of public transport (at reasonable prices) to the urban centers where a labor market and a nucleus of popular housing (casas de aluguel and "corticos") existed.[1] Thus Villas Operarias were frequent in the interior of the state. The rents charged were varied—at one extreme some firms charged at the market rate and at the other extreme did not charge their tenants. The existence of those villas in the city of Sao Paulo, was sparse, irregular and was not economically viable for the industrial firms.[2] What was more important than the latter form of housing were the huge number of one family complexes built by real estate firms, building-societies, constructors and by various investors to be rented to workers and the middle sector. The tenants of these properties were only the higher paid members of the working sector—the qualified workers and the lower middle sectors—small merchants, public servants etc. The coffee industry was dynamic enough to promote the appearance of a series of small and medium investors, linked directly or indirectly to the coffee industry, and also an emergence of a middle sector with a certain capacity to save. These various investors saw the construction of houses to rent as an excellent opportunity to invest their capital due to an instability of the industrial sector. The industrialists also invested in property, for much the same reasons, which demonstrates that their offer of housing to workers was not always due to reasons of preoccupation with supplying housing near their factories and at low prices.

The structural characteristics of the development of the economy, where the potential profits of renting houses was relatively high in relation to other investments, is fundamental to understand the predominance of "corticos" and rented houses as the housing solution of the working sectors.

Populism and the Politicization of the Social Question

The concept of populism is a term which has been most skillfully elaborated by the Latin Americans themselves. Populism, as the term is generally understood in Latin America, emerged as a response to the metropolitan revolution of the early twentieth century. After World War I different populist leaders used divergent tactics to promote mass mobilization in countries with a previously largely nonparticipant political culture. Some like Peron in Argentina were charismatic leaders. Others like Getulio Vargas were not. But all populist leaders used multiple means to build and hold their multiclass, mainly urban movements. They emphasized elections but also at times resorted to authoritarian means as a way to expand popular participation and to keep left-wing opponents, notably communists, in check. Authoritarian tendencies can be observed especially within their own parties or when in office.

Getulio Vargas came to power in 1930, after an armed insurrection which ended the political system of the so-called Old Republic. Vargas was a master at juggling with the groups that supported him in 1930. He managed the country during the 1930s by compromising between various politically and economically important groups in the country. The military were given promotion; coffee planters were not deprived of financial support; land-owners were allowed to continue exploiting the rural masses; and the middle classes were given political participation and an expanding bureaucracy in which they could find employment. As none of these groups had a power base sufficiently great to consistently impose its views on the government, Getulio Vargas succeeded in playing one against the other. But he did not solely rely on this strategy and decided that he needed a power base of his own which, from the early 1940s, he found in the relatively insignificant urban working class. Vargas' policies during the late 1930s and early 1940s were calculated to make him appear as the super-patron of the urban workers and the poor. His favours were not only of a personal patron-client relationship but also between himself and whole classes. In this new mode of operation, which Brazilian political analysts including Weffort have called "populismo", Getulio's "favours" consisted in social security and labor legislation, very advanced for his time. A new trade union structure was created in a corporatist fashion which enabled the government to manipulate the masses.

The populism that emerged in the 1940s was a combination of older traditions of local government and the twentieth century political system. In more general terms populism was a political movement arising in response to the metropolitan revolution and its urban policies. Populism stood for some sort of classless society, promising to restore the holistic nature of the society, calling for an interventionist state to regulate the economy. The main changes brought by populism were of an electoral nature. Populism stood for direct and broad elections. A second major change was the desire to enhance honest elections in the countryside. It was believed that with the growth in numbers of the urban electorate, cities should have more influence in national affairs. An important aspect of populism is its tendency to utilize clientelistic methods of recruitment. Politicians, in order to maintain the loyalty of their followers, used paid staff who worked in poor neighborhoods to recruit new voters and instruct them in balloting by distributing favours.

This is only one aspect of the not purely democratic nature of populism. Another aspect is connected with the emergence of interest groups that became important in electoral recruitment. A third and not less important aspect of democratic shortcoming was the charismatic nature of the leadership which considerably eroded the representativeness of populism. The authoritarian nature of populism became dominant from 1937 to 1945. Authoritarianism as it appeared in the 1930s, was exercised chiefly by the army. The suspension of constitutional rights, the indefinite outcome of elections and the curtailment of other forms of representativeness were justified by the claim that social peace was under danger.

The Period of Rent Control and Tenancy Laws

The intervention of the state in the housing question from the dictatorship of Getulio Vargas onwards did not limit itself to the creation of saving schemes for housing in the institutes of pensions destined to construct or finance the construction of houses for its members or the creation of the "Fundacao da Casa Popular" (The Foundation for Popular Housing). Much more important was the view that the state should be responsible for the guarantee of a minimum housing standard for the working classes at costs compatible to their low income. As we saw in the previous chapter the private market was not in a position to meet the needs of the popular housing market. The private building industry did not have sufficient yield for the capital applied in popular housing, because the people on low income did not have sufficient means to rent or acquire an adequate house. This vicious circle had grave housing consequences.

In this new milieu, the state intervened in the rental housing market through the various tenancy laws which were the most significant measures taken by the state in the housing question during the period up to 1964. The diverse tenancy laws legislated between 1942 and 1964, as they restricted the value of the rent, caused not only a complete change in the relations between property owners and tenants but also in the production of housing for the lower income groups. Renting houses was the most usual practice until then in Sao Paulo and Brazil. The majority of the population in 1940 resided in rented housing (nearly 70 percent in Sao Paulo) even though in this era the peripheries of the city were already inhabitated. In analysing the significance of the "freezing" of rents between 1942 and 1964, we will first describe the conditions of "tenancy laws" in 1942. The political situation created by the Revolution of 1930 and the emergence of the "Populist" state is of fundamental importance for the adoption of the "tenancy laws"—in

certain cases suspension of property rights—a measure that is characterized by the permanent intervention of government in housing
policy. The crisis of the oligarchic regime in 1929–30 created the
necessity for the formation of a new power structure as was analysed
by Francisco Weffort.[3]

> Weffort concluded: the conditions in which the Revolution proceeded did
> not succeed in solidly establishing the basis for the new power . . . neither
> of the great forces (the middle classes and the peripherical oligarchics)
> possessed conditions to constitute itself in the fundamentals of the new
> structure of the state. They succeeded in dislocating the political repre-
> sentation of the coffee industry, but not coffee itself as a decisive basis
> in the economy.[4]

The new politicians in power did not represent directly the groups that
dominated the basic economy. Thus, for the first time in Brazilian
history, a situation occurs where none of the economic groups exclusively dominates the political power. This situation creates the necessity
for the state to legitimate itself, but neither of the participant groups
in power could offer itself as a basis for legitimacy of the state. Under
these circumstances the urban masses appear as the only unique source
for legitimacy (after 1945).

Thus, Getulio Vargas manipulated the popular urban masses, creating
a series of measures that would legalize the social questions and recognize the masses' rights to demand revendication. The new measures
not only demonstrated Vargas' "social intentions", but also gave the
state the capacity to control the working class trade unions, the unions'
legislation and the sindicates' structure. The tenancy laws, legislated by
the "Estado Novo" (New State) was a measure that would apparently
captivate the popular sectors. We will now try to analyse the different
interests involved in the rental market. The actual "freezing" of the
rent was enforced in August 1942.

It is possible to see the tenancy laws as part of two general policies:
one, the prevention of increase, or even reduction of the cost of reproducing the labor force, the other, channelling internal resources to the
industrial sector. During this period not only were the tenancy laws
trying to guarantee minimum housing conditions at low prices as part
of a general government policy, but also for example, there was an
attempt to subsidize food prices. In 1946, a state agency—"Servico
Social da Industria"—was created with the objective of distributing
basic food products at reduced prices to industry workers. In this
perspective of trying to reduce the labor costs of large scale industry
by reducing the reproduction costs of that labor power it is possible to

understand the existence of the tenancy laws for a period of twenty years. The "freezing" of rents for such a long period is analysed as an instrument defending popular economic policy; destruction of an unproductive class (urban land owners); as a measure of controlling the cost of reproducing labor power; as an instrument of the economic policy to accelerate the growth rate of industry; as a way of legitimating the populist state.

Early Attempts at Institutionalising Public Housing

Created by legislation on the 1st of May 1946, the "Foundation for Popular Housing" was the first national agency exclusively conceived for the provision of housing for the low income sectors. The different institutes of pension funds, through their building investment accounts, provided housing at a national level but only to their members. Juscelino Kubitschek was introduced to the idea of creating a national housing agency by a successful building contractor of popular housing (later he became the first director of the "Foundation") whose projects were financed by the "Institute of Pensions for Industry" (IAPI). Together they persuaded President Dutra about the political advantages of this plan. Political considerations were seen as heavily influencing the decision to create this new housing agency. During this period, the Communist party was rising with strong support of the popular working classes in the big cities. In the elections for the "constitutional congress" the Communist party won seats for fourteen deputies and one senator, bringing up 9 percent of the electorate. The expressive voting for a previously unknown candidate for the Presidential elections (Fiuza) with 600,000 votes increased the worries of the governing elites.[5]

The government decided in this era of uncertainty, to declare the communist party and its parliamentary gains of 1947 illegal. It also tried to win the sympathy of the popular sectors by the introduction of new social policies. The "Foundation" was one of the first examples of this new strategy. This new agency to confront the housing problems was given the possibility of acting in complementary areas such as financing sewage works; water works; the supply of electrical energy; social assistance to improve the living conditions of laborers and also to finance the construction industry; research on methods and processes of cheapening the construction; finance construction under initiative or responsibility of the municipalities, state or private industries who built popular housing for sale at low prices to laborers without a profit objective.[6] Another novelty of this organization was the introduction of rural housing. All these different issues dealt by the agency reflected the perception that it was impossible to confront the housing problem without infrastructure and basic sanitation investments. It was also necessary to stimulate the production of construction materials and modernise the municipalities by training personnel.

All these proposed functions were disproportional to the political power and resources of the "Foundation for Popular Housing". It was not a question of technical, administrative and financial constraints which made it difficult to meet all these proposed objectives. The "Foundation" had a lack of political backing, as will be discussed later on. It did not have enough resources, and had no support from the states or legislation to give it a monopoly on a critical issue or put it an advantageous position to negotiate with the municipalities. The Ministry of Labor, Industry and Commerce, legislated in May 1952 a decree limiting the extent of performance of the former agency in the sectors of waterworks, sewage, electrical energy and social assistance.

The initial intention of the housing policy was to redistribute—those that would purchase a more expensive property would be subsidizing the less favoured but later on it was changed to an obligatory contribution of 1 percent of the value of purchased houses with a price above Cr$100,000. This intention to maintain the financial redistribution was not fulfilled due to two basic reasons:

1. The purchaser had a strong incentive to falsify the real value of his purchase.
2. The states who collected the taxes did not always transfer them to the "Foundation".

As this tax was ineffective and politically wasteful, it was substituted in November 1951 by declining financial allocations for the next ten years. The "Foundation" became more dependent and had to dispute with other partners for financial resources. Initially, construction was carried out by handing out contracts or by direct administration of projects.[7] Through the years the latter was dropped in favour of the former. Construction by the "Fundacao da Casa Popular", itself in the initial period of its existence, was justified by the need to familiarize its personnel with the problems of constructing low cost complexes. Since 1952, a method was developed to hand out contracts with the objective of lowering the costs of housing units while protecting the smaller and medium regional contractors. In a new version, as suggested by Kubitschek, in projects of more than fifty units, half of the work would be handed out to the "winning" contractor and the other half divided between the three best qualified construction contractors. The "Foundation" was the agency responsible for developing and designing the architectural projects. The land plots as well as the infrastructure works were carried out and donated by the municipalities. The latter agency decided on the location of the construction projects by analysing the viability of the implementation of the complexes, taking into consideration the necessities of the location, the patronage and the support of the municipalities. Technical aspects were not always the main factor in the decisions carried out.[8]

Clientelism and the Popular Housing Foundation

The legislation of the "Foundation" limited the population to whom housing was available. It referred to Brazilians and foreigners with more than ten years of residence in the country and with no private housing. There was also a preference for the acquisition or construction of housing according to the following proportions:

a. Laborers in particular activities—60 percent
b. Public servants—20 percent
c. Other persons—20 percent

Later other criteria were incorporated—those of income and size of family. Although these criteria allowed medium income families to purchase low cost housing, the latter did not find the popular housing suitable to their social position thus the "loopholes" in the legislation were not used. Income stopped being a criteria for selection and the selection of candidates was not always one of an "impersonal character". Clientelism was one of the characteristics of the public housing market as demand outpaced supply. According to Azevedo, another indicator of clientelistic pressures of the era was the existence of a kind of 'technical reserve', consisting of a small number of units in each complex, not subject to the former criteria of distribution.[9] As the housing agency was subject to political pressures, financial problems, no stable income or resources, it did not have the capability to reach a stage of institutional maturity and to commit itself to firm objectives. It was also subject to the transitory characteristics of its directors.

Significant to the analysis of public housing policies of this national agency was the spatial distribution of projects and complexes. Where were they situated? Which regions and states benefited? Which were prejudiced? By which criteria were these decisions taken? Did it respond to the localization priorities of low income housing? To which extent did the political factors influence the decisions?

By analysing the number of constructed units by size of city in 1950 (see Table 2.1) we find that the big urban centers (with a population of at least 50,000) were allocated an unproportional number of units—

TABLE 2.1 <u>The Foundation for Popular Housing</u>. Number of houses
constructed by size of cities until 31st of December 1960

Size of the City	Houses	%
1000000 +	9400	55
50000 - 100000	2200	13
20000 - 50000	2600	15
10000 - 20000	1100	7
5000 - 10000	900	5
Up to 5000	800	5
Total	17000	100

68 percent. The medium and small cities, benefited from 32 percent
of the public housing units. Although it apparently looks as if the
criteria of the spatial localization were consistent with the housing
needs of the country, big cities needed housing more urgently. But
nearly half of the housing units constructed were located in cities of
less than 20,000 inhabitants. Azevedo concludes that this large number
of units in the small cities can be explained by the fact that it is
advantageous to attend to the largest possible number of clients. In
this sense, the larger the number of cities cared for, the larger the
political dividends achieved.

The distribution of units by region (see Tables 2.2 and 2.4) is noted
by the heavy bias to the South East, where 70 percent of the housing
units were constructed, while the South and the North East had respectively, 5 percent and 14 percent of the supply. The Mid-West had
higher supply due to the demands of the new city—Brasilia. The lack
of housing in the North East can be explained as resulting from a low
level of political expression. While the high number of units in the old
state of Guanabara can be explained by the fact that it was the capital
of Brazil, in Minas it can be explained by remembering that during
that era the President of the Republic was Juscelino Kubitschek (see
Table 2.3). On the other hand, the discrepancy in regard to the number
of units constructed in the state of Sao Paulo—due to its economical,
social and demographic weight—could be explained by the political

TABLE 2.2 The Foundation for Popular Housing. Number of Houses
            Constructed by Region (Until 31/12/1960)

Region	No. of Houses	%
South East	12000	70
North East	2300	14
Mid-West	1900	11
South	900	5
North	–	–
Total	17100	100

under-representation of the state as suggested by Simon Schwartzman.[10] In response to this discrepancy a new housing agency emerged towards the end of 1949 by the name of CECAP with state wide responsibilities in financing the construction of public housing. Later on the name of this organization was changed to CODESPAULO; the objectives and roles played by this agency will be discussed in greater detail in Chapter 3.

The Popular Housing Foundation:
Is There a Solution?

In the populist era, even though the "Foundation" appeared to be the main actor in public housing policy, it contributed only a little less than 10 percent of the total number of the houses constructed by the other institutions (e.g., pension funds) during that era. But not all the housing production of the other institutions and pension funds were destinated to the low income sectors. Their clientele consisted of middle and high income families. We can ask why did the "Foundation" produce such a modest number of units (an average of 900 units per year)? Was there a misperception of electoral advantages of a popular housing program on a large scale, or were there limitations in implementing the policies? Mandated to cover a wide range of different areas, from providing loans to construction companies and municipalities' public works to elaborating housing policies, the "Foundation" was doomed to fail. It had no effective provisions to secure its financial basis as it depended on an ineffectual tax on the transfer of property,

TABLE 2.3 <u>FCP Number of Houses Constructed by States</u> (up to
31/12/1960)

State	No. of Houses	%
MINAS GERAIS	4200	25
R.J.	4000	24
SAO PAULO	3000	17
D.F.	1500	9
PERNAMBUCO	1000	6
R.G. DO SUL	600	3
CEARA	500	3
E. SANTO	300	2
EX-R. JANEIRO	300	2
R.G. DA NORTE	200	1
PARAIBA	200	1
GOIAS	200	1
SANTA CATARINA	200	1
PARANA	100	1
BAHIA	100	1
SERGIPE	100	1
MATO GROSSO	200	1
PIAUI	100	1
MARANHAO	50	0
ALAGOAS	50	0
TOTAL	16900	100

TABLE 2.4 Regions of Brazil

Regions of Brazil	Area (km2)	Area in %	Population 1960	Population 1970	Total
North (a)	3,581,180	42	2,601,000	4,485,000	4
Northeast (b)	1,548,672	18	22,429,000	33,642,000	30
Southeast (c)	942,935	11	31,100,000	47,703,000	42
South (d)	577,723	7	11,873,000	20,494,000	18
Central-West (e)	1,879,455	22	3,006,000	6,885,000	6
Total	8,511,965	100	71,009,000	113,209,000	100

(a)   States: Acre, Amazonas, Para.
(b)   States: Maranhao, Piaui, Rio Grande do Norte, Paraiba, Alagoas, Sergipe, Bahia.
(c)   States: Minas Gerais, Espirito Santo, Rio de Janeiro, Sao Paulo.
(d)   States: Parana, Santa Catarina, Rio Grande do Sul.
(e)   States: Mato Grosso do Norte, Mato Grosso do Sul, Goias Federal District.

compulsory loans from the IAPIs and ad hoc budget resources. It also had to face an inflationary environment that characterised the "Populist Republic" as well as an overstaffed organizational structure. In the fifties, members of the Brazilian Labor Party (PTB) and to a less extent, by politicians from the Social Democratic Party (PSD) exploited the "Foundation" in a marked clientelistic fashion. In 1953, financial problems led to a plan, which was never implemented, to create a bank which would be controlled by the FCP. The "Foundation" had to compete with powerful IAPIs' bureaucrats for resources from the Ministry of Labor as it was faced with the political inviability of taxing the propertied classes. This model of subsidized public housing was without yield on the investment. The problem with the populist approach to popular housing was not one of subsidizing the construction, as happens in many regimes, but in the subsidizing of nearly all the total cost. The change in housing policy would occur only with the creation of the Brazilian National Housing Bank in 1964.

The Federal Housing System:
1964 and Beyond

Urban policy in Brazil started with the foundation of the BNH in 1964. The pre-1964 era had been rather amateurish in relation to public housing policy. While in the period 1890 to 1964 only 17,000 housing units were constructed more than half a million units were built during the two decades of military regime. It is only with the creation of a federal housing system that the co-optation of the middle sectors by the government became institutionalized. The military regime recognized that investments of many kinds were needed for development but frequently implied that one kind was of essential importance—the provision of state housing for the urban middle sectors who supported them in an era of economic crisis. For the middle sectors the acquisition of their own housing had an enormous appeal and this became a central policy of the post-1964 regime in a sense of widening the support and legitimacy. By creating a federal housing bank (BNH), the government would be able to control from the center the allocation of a crucial resource (see Figure 2.1).

Political and Economic Background

The period from September 1961 to March 1964 marked years of crisis in Brazil. The military were deeply divided over the Goulart government. For the second time, the military nationalist segment of the officer corps received open support from the Presidential palace. The growing debate over the political direction of the regime had politicized students, labor union members and peasants. The drift to the left accelerated with President Goulart signing publicly two decrees. One nationalized all private oil refineries; the second stated that "under-utilized" properties of over 1200 acres located within six miles of federal highways or railways and land near federal dams would be liable to expropriation.

By contrast to earlier episodes in Brazil's political history the group brought to power by the 1964 coup drew its support from all elements of opposition to Goulart. This heterogeneous group aimed firstly at restoring confidence in the country's economy, and secondly at outlining a new strategy to achieve peace in the political arena and confidence in the economy, offering an alternative body of policies. Ever since its foundation in 1949, the Escola de Guerra had been elaborating an economic and political strategy for Brazil. Their model of national

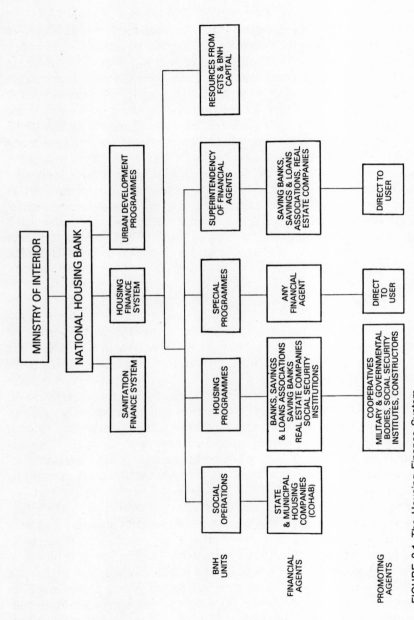

FIGURE 2.1 The Housing Finance System

development was closely linked to the new regime's concept of national security. Over the years the college had educated about two thousand military and civilian students who shared a common ideology. The preoccupation with the concept of "national security" was strengthened in the years of the Cold War. Even after the 1964 coup discussions were taken up on national "development" and its relation to "security" rather than on the more technical military issues. Security and development, the two central concepts, were seen as inextricably linked. The role of the state in national development was one of vital importance, emphasizing the role of centralization and above all rational planning as national objectives. All these concepts of national power were closely linked to the security objectives.

With the fall of the Goulart government, Castello Branco entrusted two distinguished experts with the formulation and execution of the economic policy which he proposed to adopt. These were Octavio Gouvea de Bulhoes, whom he appointed Minister of Finance, and Roberto Campos, former Ambassador to Washington, whom he placed in charge of the new Ministry of Economic Planning and Coordination. The economic team headed by Roberto Campos turned to the stabilization and restructuring of the country's monetary and fiscal policies to establish a base for economic takeoff and increased productivity. After three months of work, Campos submitted to Congress on 14 August 1964 a recovery plan which was published the following November under the title "Economic Action Plan of the Government", 1964–66, (P.A.E.G). The five main objectives were:

1. Gradually to reduce the rate of inflation to arrive at a tolerable situation of the order of 10 percent annually in 1966.
2. To increase the rate of growth of the economy to 6 or 7 percent per annum achieved during previous years.
3. To smooth out disparities between sectors of the economy and regions of the country, and also tensions due to social disequilibrium, by improving living conditions.
4. To create, through an intensive investment policy, viable conditions of productive employment sufficient to absorb the increasing inflow of labor.
5. To correct the tendency to balance of payments deficits.

At first sight these objectives may appear modest, but it should not be forgotten that during the first quarter of 1964 inflation had reached a staggering 25 percent and that the population was growing at approximately 3 percent per annum. Other measures were also drafted in the P.A.E.G to accelerate economic growth: intensification of public and private investment; introduction of foreign capital; a systematic export policy; reform of the agricultural sector both in production and marketing; and finally a top-priority housing program. Perhaps the major accomplishment of the P.A.E.G lies not so much in the attainment of specific goals as in the major concentrated effort that was made in the direction of institutional reforms and modernisation. Those reforms were to be economic and social (fiscal, agrarian and housing) and instrumental (banking and administrative).

> Reforms were the passion of the President, who believed that through them the country would change and improve. In the short run, he gave an impetus to the housing reform, that absorbed the manual labor that was temporarily unemployed because of the recession; the fiscal reform, that would be implemented in two stages; the bank reform; the agricultural reform; and also the administrative reform.[11]

Each reform required the Congress's ratification. The initial phase of attending to the housing problem was one in which the Congress approved the foundation of the BNH, the SERFHAU (Servico Federal de Habitacao e Urbanismo) and the National Housing Plan. The National Housing Plan not only intended to construct housing but also to finance a quarter of a million units in the first forty months. The "ideology" behind the Plan was to create employment and stimulate sectors of the economy, particularly civil construction which had hardly invested since the government "froze" housing rents in 1942. Lack of investment in civil construction, because of the rental policy and increasing inflation, influenced the level of supply and put pressures on rents. It is unecessary to emphasize that for the middle sectors the acquisition of private property had a tremendous appeal and this became a central policy of the post-1964 regime in a sense of widening the support and legitimacy.

The President's personal intervention in the ratification of the legislation related to public housing succeeded in maintaining monetary correction and creating new institutions such as societies for real-estate credit, the mortgage market, loan and savings associations and "Housing Cooperatives". The President's intervention was rooted in the orthodox recognition that any type of development process has to be based on savings and market considerations. According to Castello Branco's administration the first requirement for rapid and sustained economic growth was a high rate of savings. Interested parties such as the Central Bank tried unsuccessfully through Congress to oppose several of the latter propositions but the President used his "veto powers" to endorse the legislation.

In selecting a President for the BNH, Castello Branco had to choose between competing proposals of organizing the housing finance system. Roberto Campos favoured an approach which would secure a stable influx of resources for the BNH by indexing housing loans to the inflation rate. In his view this would revitalize the construction industry so as to counterbalance the anti-inflationary policies implemented by the new government while curbing consumption by channelling savings into housing schemes. The Finance Minister's (Campos) orientation was decidedly of the monetarist school. In connection with IPEA (Instituto de Pesquisas Economicas e Aplicadas) and American advisors the latter based his housing proposals primarily on fiscal rather than institutional policies as a way of getting the economy moving again. Carlos Lacerda, on the other hand, suggested that the President should choose the approach put forward by Sandra Cavalcanti, a Professor and the representative of the UDN in the Legislative Assembly of Guanabara. Cavalcanti was politically a "protege" of the governor (Lacerda) and had practical experience in housing policy through her work at the "COHAB Guanabara" (Companhia de Habitacao) and as Lacerda's first Secretary of Social Services. The President supported Cavalcanti's proposals which emphasized the need for the new regime to legitimize itself vis-a-vis the urban popular sector. In her plan not only would housing loans be subsidized by the BNH, but only State banks would operate the real estate credit societies. The manipulation of the State banks would enable the reinforcement of her group's political leverage. Cavalcanti's plans also complied with Castello Branco's vision of his presidency as a transitional stage towards a civilian regime. Another important reason for choosing Calcavanti was the fact that a woman was nominated for the first time to such a high governmental positon.[12]

The Growth of State Involvement in the Economy

It is important to understand the role of economic growth in Brazil after 1964 since it played an important part in securing political support for the regime and allowed for a tremendous expansion of the export capacity of the economy. Intensive import substitution industrialization programs characterized Brazilian government policy in the decade of the 1950s. Government policy worked to protect Brazilian industry; emphasized investments in infrastructure; created special incentives for foreign capital; and established a powerful development bank. High real growth rates were the outcome in 1950–61. The impact of industrialization on the economy was enormous. The governmental scheme created distortions affecting various sectors, increasing regional inequality; reducing investment in agriculture, leading to a decline in world prices for traditional exports, strain in the balance of payments, and a more concentrated income distribution. Whereas the period of the 1950s was characterized by a GDP growth of more than 6 percent and industrial production growth of 10 percent, the 1960–67 period witnessed stagnation. The replacement of the Goulart government by the Military Republic witnessed changes in priorities—restoring the economy to higher levels of production. The period between 1961 to 1964 had been a time of hyperinflation, disequilibrium in the balance of payments, increasing short term external indebtedness, and a sharp reduction in the rate of output growth. Roberto Campos economic plans aimed at stabilizing and restructuring fiscal and monetary policies to establish a firmer base for economic takeoff.

The new regime believed that in order to restore economic growth it was necessary to control inflation, to modernize capital markets and to eliminate price distortions. Investment in state-owned industries and infrastructural projects was essential to the success of the government's policy. During this period inflation was brought under control and distortions in the price structure were considerably reduced. Government expenditures were curtailed, tax revenues increased, credit tightened and wages held down. The new government emphasized in its first years a need for stabilization and structural reforms in the financial markets. Policy actions, such as curtailment of government expenditure, increased tax revenues, tightening of credit, and limits on wage increases, led to a steady decline in the government budget deficit. The repression of the trade unions and the consolidation of an authoritarian political system enabled the government to pursue a strict wage policy. As government expenditure was controlled, government salaries declined. All these factors contributed to the achievement of a decelerating rate of inflation. Meanwhile, buoyant tax and social security revenues served to transform the government into an important source of savings in the economy. In 1965, the introduction of a capital market law encouraged the establishment of investment banks to underwrite new issues. Since the late 1960s social security and retirement funds, a system of forced savings, provided a large proportion of the resources for these governmental credit institutions (e.g. the FGTS). All these savings were indexed as was the newly created BNH which was allowed to issue index linked bonds and loans. Although the stagnation evident in the Brazilian economy by 1962 continued after the coup of 1964 and lasted until 1968, government investment expenditures were never cut back as existing infrastructure projects were continued.

Reorientation of Housing Policy, 1964–83

Government intervention in the housing market requires state expenditure, both for capital outlays and revenue outlays. The scale of these outlays reflects not only changes in political power but also the national economic conjuncture and its theoretically perceived relationship with state expenditure. Before the acceptance of John Maynard Keynes' theories, the orthodox response to the crisis was to cut state expenditure. In the golden age of Keynes, during the two decades following the Second World War, changes in the flow of state expenditure were seen both as a means of regulating aggregate demand, positively or negatively, and a way of shifting productive resources from one economic activity to another. The Brazilian planners of the 1950s and early 1960s followed the intellectual leader of a group of economists (Furtado, appointed director of the BNDE in 1958 and later minister of planning) in the belief that economic development in Brazil required basic "structural" changes in the economy, which could best be achieved through planning and implementation of plans by the state. The change of government in 1964 brought differences of various degrees in the internal organization of the Planning Ministry but the basic belief of an intense commitment to state intervention in the economy did not change. Roberto Campos followed in terms of actual operation of the planning ministry in virtually the same fashion as the Furtado ministry, with a single planning director at the top reporting directly to the President. (In the last decade state expenditure and monetary developments have been perceived as closely intertwined and the monetarist response to inflation has been to attempt to restrain expenditure in order to control domestic credit expansion at the same time as interest rate policy has raised revenue subsidies. The effect was to reduce dramatically the balance of resource expenditure and gift expenditure on state housing in the five years after 1972–73).

The Initial Role of the BNH

The initial role of the BNH was to solve housing problems in Brazil. While the SFH attributes the basic function of promoting construction and the acquisition of houses especially for the lower income sectors, the BNH's function was to orientate, discipline and control the SFH of which it was an element. The federal government, through the Ministry of Planning, formulated the national housing and land policy, coordinated the action of the statutory bodies and oriented private initiative in stimulating the construction of public housing and financing house purchasing especially for lower income sectors. The federal government would intervene in the housing market through the following:

1. The BNH
2. The SFH
3. Federal saving associations (Caixas Economicas Federais).

The BNH was closely bound to the Ministry of Internal Affairs and would have its own judicial personality, assets and administrative autonomy, with the advantage of judiciary immunity. The Bank could install agencies in the whole of Brazil and use commercial bank facilities in localities without agencies. The main functions of the BNH were:

1. To orientate, discipline and control the SFH.
2. To initiate the creation of savings and their distribution to the SFH.
3. To discipline the access of agencies for housing credit to the national capital market.

The BNH was created to serve as executive agent of the Housing Finance System (SFH) whose goal was to promote the construction and acquisition of homes, especially by the lower income sectors. The bank is the guarantor and ultimate repository of voluntary savings generated through the Brazilian Saving and Loan System (SBPE). The system has been successful in concentrating a large proportion of popular savings by periodically increasing deposits to adjust for inflation ("indexing") and adding to this a substantial interest rate. In 1967, the BNH acquired access to a vast pool of compulsory savings through the creation of the Guaranteed Employment Fund (FGTS). The fund has the ostensive purpose of creating a patrimony for the worker and his family and is formed by employers' contributions totalling 8 percent of their payroll. Deposits in FGTS are also indexed to the cost of living and receive annual interest of up to 6 percent. BNH acts both as recipient and manager of the fund. The size of the liquid assets BNH receives through the voluntary and compulsory saving systems now exceeds the total budgets of several federal ministries.[13]

By 1973, they represented close to 6 percent of the gross domestic product. These resources are also impressive in absolute terms: in 1973, BNH had control over approximately US $6 billion, by the end of 1975 the figure had grown to over US $16 billion. Of the latter figure, 40 percent corresponded to voluntary savings (FGTS), and nearly a third to resources already accumulated by the bank and the SBPE plus other minor funds. The fact that BNH became an economic giant is not fortuitous, for it is the instrument of the national state in achieving a complex array of goals. The bank is the prime agent of the government in two fundamental "social" areas: housing and the generation of popular employment. The bank's initial mandate was to meet a national housing deficit estimated at eight million units.

It was charged, in the words of a former President of the Republic, to "propitiate greater security, comfort, and well-being to the families of most scarce resources and contribute to a better distribution of income and a reduction of regional income inequalities (Garrastuzu, Medici)".[14]

To meet this goal, BNH organized a house construction program in the "social interest" area. At the same time, however, the bank was charged with the task of stimulating employment among the urban unskilled and semiskilled workers. Roberto Campos, the former Finance Minister summarized the two-pronged social strategy by BNH:

Favouring home ownership by the less favoured classes while stimulating simultaneously the absorption of unskilled manpower by the civil con- stuction industry, the housing policy contributes to the achievement of two basic objectives of the government program: to insure . . . oppor- tunities for productive employment to the continuously increasing man- power flowing into the labor market; to alleviate regional and sectoral economic inequalities and the tensions created by social disequilibrium through improvements in the human condition.[15]

Mario Trinidade, one of the first presidents of the BNH (1966–1971), understood that the ultimate rationale of these social objectives was to reduce the dangers of social tension among the urban masses and those arising from the exchange between the urban and rural masses.[16]

Financing Urban Development and Industrial Expansion

In Brazil, the process of industrialization occurred over a relatively brief span of time. Unlike either Britain or the US, capitalist firms in Brazil did not, by and large, undergo a lengthy period of expansion. Instead, many of the firms operating in Brazil sprang up in the 1950s as full blown enterprises established to produce certain commodities which the Brazilian state had targeted as priority needs for development. Overall, there was no lengthy process of innovation spurred on by competition and market forces. As a result of the preponderant role of the State in the accumulation process, a hybrid form of capitalist development has emerged in Brazil.[17] The history of capitalist devel-

opment in Brazil differs substantially from those nations where industrial production was the chief source of capital accumulation. At the
beginning of the twentieth century, accumulation was based primarily
on export production. Beginning in the 1950s, the structure of industrial
production started to change considerably. In 1949, the industrial sector
displaced agriculture in terms of value added. By 1973, the value of
industrial production was twice that of agriculture. Furthermore the
rate of investment in industry rose dramatically.

> The development of an advanced industrial sector, from 1964 onwards,
> was achieved under the control of monopoly capital. Throughout this
> process, the Brazilian state has played a crucial role. Particularly since
> 1964, the state has favoured development (but especially growth) at almost
> any price. One of the initial problems confronting Brazil in the 1950s
> was the absence of an infrastructure capable of supporting advanced
> multinational enterprises.[18]

In creating this infrastructure, the state simultaneously created a market
for the industrial products. State support of industries in the monopoly
sector was viewed as the best way to foster long term economic
development and capital accumulation. By analysing trends in the
federal budget and specifically public expenditure in urban development,
through time, we can observe the state's political and economic intervention in the industrial sector. During the actual stage of capitalist
development, the monopolistic corporations tend to depend on state
investment for their expansion.

With the accumulation of funds through compulsory and voluntary
savings the original objectives of the SFH were adjusted not only to
include investment in public housing but to turn its attention to the
growth of cities. Since the early 1970s the federal housing agency began
to invest in physical infrastructure (e.g., water supply and sewerage
systems) as experience showed the scarcity of municipal and state
resources and expenditure in the latter. During this period the government's policies also emphasized a need for economic development (but
especially growth) at almost any price. The BNH began during this era
to revise the distribution of its budget. By looking at the expenditure
side of the budget one notices an emphasis towards public investment
in urban development as opposed to a previous commitment to investment in housing. Up to 1978, the total expenditure of the BNH on
housing was on average 70 percent; on urban development 25 percent
(of this figure half was invested on sanitation). In 1979/81 two thirds
of the budget was allocated to housing and one third to urban development. During the period of 1982–83, an even higher proportion of

TABLE 2.5 Housing Financial System - Number of Units Financed by
Region: 1964-1975

REGION	SBPE (1)	RECON (3)	SOCIAL INTEREST AREA (2)	TOTAL
South East	370000	76500	293000	739500
North East	55000	14700	131000	200700
South	55500	12300	86000	153800
Centerwest	12100	3000	65000	80100
North	14000	1000	24000	39000
Others	-----	21000	8000	29000
Total	506600	128500	607000	1242100

(1) Sistema Brasileiro de Poupanca e Emprestimo

(2) Housing for the Low Income

(3) Financing or refinancing for consumers of building materials

the total expenditure was allocated to urban development. This trend
towards investing larger proportions of public housing funds on infrastructure in the highly industrialized urban centers of the South East
region of Brazil is clearly part of state policy to support industries
during the stages of capitalist development in which corporations depend on state investment for their expansion. By analysing Table 2.5
on the distribution of finance for housing units in the various regions
of Brazil one can clearly see the emphasis of allocating a high proportion
of funds to the industrialized regions.

Not only is there a trend towards investing social capital to support
industrial development but substantial amounts of BNH funds were
invested directly in industrial projects. This happens when the government is unable to financially support its public commitments. For
example, on 26 April 1973 President Stroessner of Paraguay and President Medici of Brazil signed the Itaipu Treaty to build the largest
hydro-electric power project in the world with an installed capacity of
12,600 megawatts.[19]

As the cost of Itaipu escalated from an initial estimate of two billion
US$ in 1972, to over ten billion US$ in the early 1980s, the Brazilian
government which had committed itself to finance nearly all the project,

had to look for new foreign and domestic sources for funding. One of the unofficial sources was the BNH which diverted substantial amounts of its budget to this "jumbo" project but also to others in which Brazil invested heavily in the 1970s. They include (apart from Itaipu) the Tucurui hydro station (US $6 billion); the Acominas steel mill (US $5 billion and idle) and the railway to take its output to the coast; new metro systems for both Rio de Janeiro and Sao Paulo; the Carajas iron mining project; and an expensive nuclear power program. All these projects are part of a government policy for economic development and growth. At first the continuation of these projects depended largely on the generous support of foreign bankers; since the latter decided to lessen their financial risks and withdraw some of their funds, the government has had to divert resources from agencies, such as the BNH, to meet the rising costs of all of these giant industrial projects.

Regional and Inter-Regional Distribution of Public Housing

The functioning of the Brazilian political system is influenced by important non-political determinants. These provide over time a framework of the characteristic configurations of power in the various regimes in Brazil. Among the most important of these determinants are national geography, the distinctive regional bias in national settlement patterns, the demographic aspects of national growth, and educational and social developments. Each of these has contributed to the shaping of the present public housing distribution pattern in Brazil. The diversity of Brazil is exemplified by its regions: each represents a particular aspect of the cultural, historical, economic and ethnic diversity of the whole. The unity of Brazil has often seemed superficial, and indeed in colonial times "Brazil" was little more than a loosely connected series of coastal settlements. The first decades of the Empire, after independence from Portugal in 1822, were spent in repressing separatist movements in the North East and South. While the Empire provided a central focus for national unity, the power and influence of the regions remained a fact of life in the nineteenth century. During the Old Republic (1889–1930) the federal government served as little more than a clearing house for regional political and economic decisions. The Vargas era (1930–45) saw a steady diminution in the influence of the states and regions. The 1946 Republic (1946–64) saw a compromise with the regional phenomenon. The states were granted some autonomy, but the powers of the federal government, on balance, outweighed the combined force of the states. Since the Revolution of 1964, the central government has effectively curbed any show of independence emanating from the state governments. The centralization of power in Brasilia is the clear trend.

The Significance of Regionalism

Given the distinctive patterns of colonization, settlement and economic growth during the colonial period—which were accompanied by the accumulation of social influence as well as economic wealth by the dominant families of the region—regionalism became and remains a potent variable in discussing politics.

The industrialization scheme of the government in the decade of the 1950s created serious distortions in the economy. Regional inequality increased; agriculture received little new investment; income distribution became more concentrated; there were intensive internal migrations. The latter distortion during the period of 1950–60 can be characterized as one of intense migration from the poor North East to the economically developing areas of the central south. This migration pattern occurred during a period of great economic and industrial growth in the latter regions. According to a recent study in the less developed countries, metropolitan growth is the direct consequence of rural-urban migration. During the decade 1950–1960, such migration constituted 60 percent of urban growth. This figure is likely to come down to 42 percent during the decade 1980–1990.[20] The metropolitan regions of the developing countries contain much of the modern sector of the national economies and hence attract the largest number of migrants.

It was also during this era of rapid industrialization that the Foundation for Popular Housing was founded as one of the measures taken by the government in the critical housing question. The background to the foundation of this national housing agency was political. The Communist Party during this period was rising with strong support from the working sectors in the big cities and the Dutra government tried to win the sympathy of the lower sectors by implementing social policies. In analysing the number of units constructed by size of city in the 1950s we can already identify a pattern which would intensify later on. The big urban centers were privileged—70 percent of the public housing was constructed there. The distribution of units by regions is noted by the heavy bias to the South East, where 70 percent of the units were built, while the South and North East had respectively 5 percent and 14 percent of the total supply. The Mid-West had an elevated supply due to the demands of the new city-Brasilia. The lack of housing in the North East can be explained as resulting from a low level of political expression. While the high number of units in the old state of Guanabara can be explained by two reasons. The first that Rio de Janeiro was the capital of Brazil and the second by remembering that the President of the Republic was Juscelino Kubitschek. On the other hand, the discrepancy in regard to the number of units constructed in the state of Sao Paulo—due to its economical, social and demographic weight—could be explained by the political sub-representation of the state as suggested by Simon Schwartzman.[21]

With the creation of the Federal Housing System in 1964 the new government promised to invest in public housing and to reduce the distortions of a heavily biased pattern. Although the Brazilian housing finance system has accounted for some overall redistribution between regions in favour of the poorer North East, the main bulk of the funds still goes to the industrialized South East where they were collected. Like most Latin American countries, but not as much as in Argentina, Uruguay or Venezuela, the Brazilian urban population tends to concentrate in a few large centres. By 1975, the population of metropolitan Sao Paulo and Rio de Janeiro together accounted for a fifth of the national population. Since both areas are highly urbanised, we may conclude that this represents 30 percent of the urban inhabitants (with G.S.P alone accounting for 15 percent). The South East region, although representing only 11 percent of the Brazilian territory, contained by 1970 more than 42 percent of the country's entire population and by 1980 Sao Paulo state alone contained 21 percent of Brazil's inhabitants. This region is undoubtedly the main centre of economic activity with income per head being in some areas (e.g., S.P. state) more than double that in the rest of the country. The fact that the South East has established itself as the dominant region of the process of growth and accumulation of wealth in Brazil implies indeed a relative impoverishment of other parts of the country, such as the North East. Not only does the former region bring together the most advanced sectors of industrial and agricultural production, but the vast majority of public expenditure in welfare and particularly in urban development is invested in the South East.

While most of the funds and units do go to the South East of the country the housing finance system has accounted for some overall redistribution between regions in favor of the poorer North East. But the overwhelming majority of the funds still go to the region where they were collected—the urban and industrialized South East (see Table 2.5). The housing finance system collects resources from two sources: FGTS—which is the compulsory social security fund of all registered workers, and SBPE (Sistema Brasileiro de Poupanca e Emprestimo)—which collects private, voluntary savings. The latter has grown from being a small part of the total since its promotion by BNH in 1971 to account for more than 3/4 of all resources collected in 1975. The regional collection of both FGTS and SBPE resources reflects to a great extent regional wealth and its distribution to employees, but whereas FGTS is transferable between regions, SBPE funds stay largely in the state or region where the collecting agency is based. If SBPE funds are redistributed they tend to go to the richer areas of higher market demand for housing. To some extent FGTS funds have been redistributed (via the low income housing and urban development) away from the South East towards, in particular, the North East. During the decade of the 1970s nearly 60 percent of all housing units and all resources of the BNH had been distributed to the rich urban industrial areas of the Southeast.

The 1982 elections for state government have brought a change in the distribution pattern of public expenditure on urban development. Some 56,000 posts were contested in November's elections, from senators and congressmen down to local councillors. The most important were those for the 22 state governors which, since the 1964 coup, had always been held by government men (with two exceptions in 1965).

Although the government's PDS won most governships (12 out of 22) the opposition Democratic Movement (PMDB) won most of the votes (44 percent against 42 percent for the PDS). The government retained control of the electoral college but the PMDB took governships of the two key states, Sao Paulo and Minas Gerais, which between them account for almost half of Brazil's GNP.[22]

In the state of Rio de Janeiro, the left wing Democratic Labor Party drew some consolation from the gubernatorial victory of Leonel Brizola (the PDT won only 6 percent of the national votes). These recent elections introduced a new pattern: overt hostility and opposition towards the existing national regime coupled with an increase in party politics, in autonomous modes of political organization, and in changing political alignment. The South East region is now a stronghold of the PMDB and the main locus of gradual organization of the autonomous PT with its charismatic trade union leader, Luis Ignacio da Silva (Lula). The PT although it won less than 10 percent of the total votes increased its political power with a stronghold in the "ABC"—the heavy industrialized region of Sao Paulo state. The increase in the opposition's power especially in the South East has required a change in the "rules of the game". The federal government has increased the politicization of state resources and encouraged patrimonial links while constantly tinkering with electoral laws. There has been a changing trend toward investing more in urban development projects in the "pro-government" North East states. In the race for the Congress nomination for the 1985

Presidential elections, Mario Andreazza—the Minister for Internal Affairs (who also administers the national housing program)—had sought support from North East Senators by diverting substantial BNH resources towards the "development" of this region.

International Lending Institutions
and Housing Policy

Although the International Bank for Reconstruction and Development, now known exclusively as the "World Bank", began operating formally in 1946, it was only after 1973 that the Bank diversified the sectoral allocation of its funds away from an almost exclusive concern with funding projects of basic economic infrastructure toward projects explicitly devoted to the alleviation of poverty in less-developed countries. A major policy initiative of the American government which was particularly illustrative of poverty-oriented emphases, anticipated by many years the World Bank's newer concerns. The Alliance for Progress, launched by President Kennedy in 1961 marked a fundamental reorientation of Washington's policy toward Latin America. It was perhaps the most systematic effort to exert U.S. influence on Latin American states. While the primary objective of the Alliance was an increase in economic growth rates, its second objective was a more equitable distribution of national income. The Alliance aimed at reforms in the region's economic and social systems and proposed specific policy reorientations in housing, agriculture, health and education.

During the fiscal years 1961 and 1962, Brazil received US$358 millions from the Alliance. Nearly 14,000 houses were constructed with USAID finance in the states of Guanabara, Rio Grande do Sul and Minas Gerais. These states were strongholds of the UDN, a party established in 1945 as a coalition of forces which opposed the pro-Vargas parties. Its members comprised of local political bosses and the conservative industrialists and financiers who in 1961 managed to provide a bandwagon for the successful presidential candidacy of the independent Janio Quadros. In Rio de Janeiro the U.S.A government financed the planning and execution of three housing projects on the far outskirts of the city. These projects housed "favelados" that were relocated from high value properties in the center. Sao Paulo, a state dominated by the P.S.P (Partido Social Progressista), the party of Adhemar de Barros during the early 1960s, did not receive financial contributions from USAID programs.

A considerable evolution of the World Bank's involvement in the consumption and production aspects of urban projects occurred between tax years 1973 and 1981. The earliest projects had a sites-and-services emphasis. This was followed by somewhat greater emphasis on slum upgrading. The 1980s see a movement away from isolated projects towards more general urban projects. In Brazil the Bank opted for sites and services over upgrading as the latter created severe political problems. In proliferating favelas with an incredible population density, it was considerably difficult to carry out the plot demarcation that was a prerequisite of successful land titling. Not only was a time-consuming cadastral survey often needed but the entire underlying concept of land ownership was not so straightforward in some places. Although in slum-upgrading the Bank review asserts that projects in Brazil have demonstrated that it is possible to reach the first decile of the urban income distribution, the government housing agencies did not always accept this approach. They could see a payoff with new urban shelters but did not see a payoff with the upgrading of grubby slums. Undertaking poverty-oriented projects in countries with a military regime seems contrary to their political systems and economic development strategies.

Financing the System

Financing for the National Housing Bank comes equally from two sources—one forced and one voluntary. The first is the Guaranteed Employment Fund, a form of mandatory savings to which all employers contribute 8 percent of the wages earned by their employees. The accounts may be drawn upon in times of illness, disability, unemployment, or for the purchase of a house. The second is a voluntary savings from the sale of housing bonds and from the savings deposited through passbook accounts in the savings and loan system. The creation of the Fundo de Garantia do Tempo de Servico—a system of social insurance which required compulsory contributions by employed people—in September 1966, was fundamentally intended to complement the labor legislation. Specifically, in the field of unemployment, compensation and stability of employees, by trying to get around the much publicized deficiencies. Apart from that the FGTS offered new welfare conditions, through the possibility of utilizing resources in the event of prolonged unemployment, illness of the employee or members of his family, of wanting to become self-employed, and also the acquisition of housing. Thus, the newly inaugurated policy not only envisioned better relations between employees but also offered new possibilities of social and economic improvements for employees.

Since 1958, the Federal government was looking at ways of creating incentives for the employers to build up reserves destinated to cover the eventual unemployment of employees. Until 1966, the employers tried to control the situation by limiting the maximum time of employment in one firm. In order to avoid such burdensomeness of the labor legislation and to obtain better relationships between the employers and employees, the government implemented the FGTS in 1966. The policies of 1964 were aimed at reforming the housing market, modifying the tenancy laws, introducing the mechanism of monetary correction in credit operations, creating new saving schemes, establishing incentives for the construction of housing, as well as new guarantees and facilities for the purchasers. This adopted orientation enhanced the social character of the new policy, with the intention of attending specially the lower income families. Since then, it was established that it was necessary to captivate resources at low cost, in order to confront the small acquisitive power of the urban middle sectors, whose demand was considered by the new military government as of high priority.

The establishment of the FGTS came as a means of providing financial support for the latter policies. The BNH would administer the new fund and would guarantee interest rates on the accumulated real balances with a minimum of 3 percent per year and a maximum of 6 percent per year (in accordance with the length of employment of the participating employee). The FGTS rapidly became the principal source of new resources of the BNH. Statistics that refer to the years 1973 and 1974 indicate that nearly 80 percent of the value of the drafts arise out of the employees remissions. This elevated percentage denotes the principal characteristic of the FGTS: a fund of reserves for labor indemnification. An increasing use has been made of the draft rights especially in the cases of establishing a self-employed position for the worker, prolonged unemployment, illness and retirement income. The drafts for acquisition of housing were particularly significant in 1972: 3.2 percent of the total value of the withdrawals. This right of withdrawal reached a level of plenitude once the employees had been participants of the FGTS for at least a minimum of five years. As the FGTS was created in 1966, it was only in 1971 that the right to use funds to purchase housing was initiated. During the two following years the withdrawals for house purchase had relative less significance and later on increased dramatically in the first eight months of 1975. This increase was influenced by better facilities adopted as of June of that year (the alternatives of the withdrawal rights were amplified as it became possible to withdraw more than once). Since then the balance of the employees' FGTS account could be used to reduce, mortgage or liquidate the conceded loan, as well as to start a saving scheme necessary to purchase a house. All this was approved as long as the financing value did not exceed 3500 UPC.

TABLE 2.6 Deposits and Withdrawal of FGTS Funds by Income (1973)
(In Percentages)

Accumulated Distribution

No. of Minimum Monthly Salaries	Accumulative Percentage of Deposits	Total Value of Funds Withdrawn
Less than 1	7	20
1 to 2	27	52
2 to 3	41	66
3 to 5	57	79
10 to 10	74	89
10 and above	100	100

The table above demonstrates that the distribution of withdrawals by employees is rather concentrated in the lower income sectors. Workers with a monthly income of less than ten monthly salaries were responsible for nearly 90 percent of the total value of the funds withdrawn.

Table 2.6 indicates that those employed with an income below two monthly salaries deposited less than 30 percent of the FGTS's total funds, while they were responsible for more than half of the withdrawals made in 1973. In contrast to the latter the personnel that earns more than ten minimum salaries contributes to nearly 26 percent of the deposits but was responsible for only 11 percent of the withdrawals. This characteristic signifies that the rights of withdrawal (at least during one specific period) were principally used by the lower income sectors and for this reason they tend to have lesser balance accumulated in the fund. To the extent that the latter withdraw more funds because of indemnification motives the less they will be able to utilize the facilities and subsidies conceded to the programs of financement for housing. The low acquisitive power and the feeble saving capacity of the lower income sectors, has constituted one of the principal restrictions on the social character of the housing programs. If the voluntary savings of these sectors are modest or inexistent and for this reason they are forced to utilize the accumulated balances in the Fund to outlast unemployment, then the lesser their possibilities to participate in the financing for the acquisition of housing.

Composition of the Revenues and
Financial Costs of the BNH

The importance of the FGTS in the composition of annual revenues of the BNH has reached an average of nearly 50 percent in the period 1969/74. Table 2.9 shows the amount of deposits of the FGTS with the latter. This is a compulsory savings for consumers, because it goes direct to BNH as a liability. But it is also hot money for BNH because an employee may withdraw the deposit plus interest and monetary correction any time e.g., when he is temporarily unemployed or retires or when purchasing a home. Deposits as shown on Table 2.7 have increased but so have withdrawals, from 3 percent in 1967 (first full year of operation) to 44 percent (January–July of 1976). Tables 2.8 and 2.9 show the sources of and applications of funds of the BNH. The FGTS still represents the major source of funds or 70 percent in April 1976, but used to be as high as 80 percent in 1971. On the side of the application, the BNH agents have been receiving a little bit more than half of the resources. In 1971 and 1974 they accounted for 60 percent. During the first half of 1976, the percentage decreased to 55 percent, while the balance has been transferred to commercial and development banks, mainly public banks for infrastructure (urban development, sanitation and transportation, etc.).

By analysing the percentages among the BNH agents, it is clear that the BNH has not been providing the greater part of its financing to the lower income sectors or those getting finance from the COHABs and COOPHABs. In 1971, nearly 40 percent of the Bank's resources were allocated to these two institutions, but since 1972 there has been a declining trend in the financing of low income projects. At the same time by looking at the increased participation of the SCI and APE we can see that there has been an upward trend in the expenditure on high income housing programs.

Redemocratization and Social Policy: Does
Central Government Need to Control Local Spending?

The resurgence of democracy in Brazil in 1985 brought forth severe public criticisms of the Federal Housing System which led to the abolition of the BNH in November 1986. Although the BNH suffered from the fact that it was associated with the displaced military regime, it is important not to forget that the abolition occurred during a period of economic crisis. Until 1982, the BNH expanded its activities in the areas of housing, sanitation and urban development. From 1982 onwards the Brazilian housing bank entered a period of severe cuts in its

TABLE 2.7 Social Security Fund for Employees (FGTS)
(In Millions of Cr$)

PERIOD	FLOW OF THE PERIOD WITH NET				BALANCE AT END OF PERIOD WITH NET			
	DEPOSITS 1	DRAWS 2	BALANCE 3=1-2	% 2/1	DEPOSITS 4	DRAWS 5	BALANCE 6 (*)	%
1967	616	19	597	3	616	19	597	3
1868	1223	216	1007	18	1839	235	1604	13
1969	1801	573	1228	32	3640	808	2832	22
1970	2518	1005	1513	40	6158	1813	4345	29
1971	3529	1542	1987	44	9687	3355	6332	34
1972	4950	2244	2706	45	14637	5599	9038	38
1973	6820	2951	3869	43	21457	8550	12907	40
1974	9779	4184	5595	43	31236	12734	18502	40
1975	14888	6925	7963	47	46124	19659	26465	43
1976 (Jan-Jul)					57863	25251	32612	44

* 6 = 4-5

TABLE 2.8   BNH - Application of Funds (In Percentages)

Housing Financing and Refinancing Institutions	1971	1972	1973	1974	1975	1976
State Banks (and Others)	40	28	32	40	43	46
SCI	10	23	26	24	25	23
COHAB's	19	17	14	12	12	11
COOPHAB's	20	20	17	11	6	6
APE	3	7	7	9	10	10
CEF	5	3	2	2	3	3
CEE's	3	2	2	2	1	1
Total	100	100	100	100	100	100

TABLE 2.9   BNH - Source of Funds (Millions of Cr$)

Own Resources	1971	1972	1973	1974	1975	1976
Capital	957	982	2000	2750	8000	8000
Reserves	567	1545	1849	5261	4737	7086
Result of Period	29	----	505	1261	821	864
Total	1553	2527	4354	9272	13558	15949
FGTS	9813	14788	20982	32897	48413	59825
OTHERS	522	1082	1048	1902	8423	10089
TOTAL	11888	18397	26384	44073	70394	85865
FGTS/TOTAL	(82%)	(80%)	(79%)	(75%)	(69%)	(70%)

investment programs as a result of the economic recession. A sharp increase in the unemployment figures led to a massive withdrawal of FGTS funds. The FGTS was part of a housing finance system created to work in an "environment" with an average of 40 to 50 percent annual rate of inflation. With an annual rate of inflation of over 200 percent and high unemployment figures the housing finance system collapsed. House-owners who obtained a BNH mortgage during the 1983–85 period were subject to a 100 percent link to the index of living costs while the minimum monthly salary was only 80 percent linked. The high rates of inflation resulted in a sharp increase in the monthly repayments to the BNH. It was estimated that during this period an average of 60 percent of house-owners were behind schedule in repayments of mortgages. House-owners also started to appeal to the Federal Tribunal of Resources (TFR) against the BNH's mortgage policy. In February 1985, a Federal judge allowed, for the first time in two decades, house-owners to withdraw FGTS savings to repay mortgages. This decision increased the liquidity crisis of the BNH. A few months later, the Tribunal declared that it was illegal that the BNH readjust loans at rates above the rise in monthly salaries. More specifically, the TFR decided that the BNH should compensate the 3.2 million house-owners as to the repayment on mortgages since 1983. This decison alone was enough to result in the collapse of the BNH as it meant a deficit of Cr$ 40 trillion. The Brazilian federal government decided to pardon six months of monetary correction to house-owners who financed their property through the SFH. Sayad, the Minister of Planning declared that more than 40 million contributors to FGTS would also have to be compensated by the Treasury.

The crisis which the BNH faced in the 1980s resulted in a reform of the housing finance system. As of December 1986, most of the BNH's activities were transfered to the Federal Saving Bank (CEF). The new system divided the BNH's functions between two actors: the CEF and the Central Bank. The CEF would finance housing for the lower income sectors; it would also administer the FGTS; social and urban development policies. The CEF was chosen by the new civilian government to take over the functions of the BNH as it had agencies all over Brazil. Transfer of functions was envisaged by the federal government to bring large savings in adminstrative costs, although most of the BNHs 8300 employees were transferred to CEFs payroll. The Central Bank would administer the Brazilian Savings and Loans System (SBPE); the Fund for Liquidity Assistance (FAL); and the Fund for the Guarantee of Deposits and Real-Estate Credit (FGDLI). One of the objectives of this new system was to increase the rate of public investment on the so called "social interest" housing programs. According to legislation, the CEF would finance housing to a population with up to 5 minimum monthly salaries. CEF would finance mainly municipal and state housing programs. Such a situation would probably result in a higher level of autonomy of state and municipal authorities in planning housing programs.

Given the constraint of central government revenues in most non-democratic regimes in the last few years, it is important that local government develop new ways to generate revenue and allocate resources more efficiently. Local governments that have come to rely heavily on intergovernmental grants or transfers are finding it ever more difficult to provide adequate urban services. Strengthening local government finance can improve public sector efficiency and reduce the need for transfers from central to local government. The most obvious and potentially broad-based of local revenues is the property tax. A recent research of developing countries revealed that only 5 to 25 percent of local government recurrent receipts came from property taxes. Many cities lack accurate property records. In yet other countries, the collection system is inadequate and tax delinquency is high. In addition many local governments lack the autonomy to set tax rates, which as a result may not function equitably and cost-effectively. Another potential source of increasing revenues is borrowing to finance at least some of the local capital investment.[23]

Notes

1. Nabil Bondukie, "Origems do Problema da Habitacao Popular em Sao Paulo", in *Espaco e Debates* (Brazil: March/June 1982), p. 100.

2. *Ibid.*

3. Francisco Weffort, *O Populismo na Politica Brasileira* (Rio de Janeiro: Paz e Terra, 1980), p. 64.

4. *Ibid*, p. 76.

5. T. Skidmore, *Brasil: De Getulio a Castello, 1930–64* (Rio de Janeiro: Paz e Terra, 1976), p. 90.

6. Sergio Azevedo and Luis Gama de Andrade, *Habitacao e Poder* (Rio de Janeiro: Zahar, 1982), p. 21.

7. Fundacao Casa Popular, *Estatutos Aprovada Pela Portaria* (Rio de Janeiro: Ministerio de Trabalho, 1952).

8. *Atas do Conselho Tecnico da Fundacao da Casa Popular* (Rio de Janeiro: 1953).

9. Azevedo and Andrade, *op. cit.*, p. 27.

10. Simon Schwartzman, *Sao Paulo e o Estado Nacional* (Sao Paulo: Difel, 1975).

11. Luis Viana, *O Governo Castello Branco* (Brazil: J. Olympio, 1975), p. 91.

12. Another possibility is that Cavalcanti had been a close friend of the President's late wife.

13. Gabriel Bolaffi, "Habitacao e Urbanismo", in *Ensaios de Opiniao* (Brazil: Vol. 2., 1975), pp. 73–83.

14. Alejandro Portes, "Housing Policy, Urban Poverty and the State," in *Latin American Research Review*, (USA: Vol. 14, No. 2., 1979), p. 7.

15. *Ibid.*, p. 7.

16. *Ibid.*, p. 7.

17. Glen Harrisson, *Accumulation, Technological Change and Transformation of the Labour Process* (USA: Library of Congress, 1983).

18. *Ibid.*

19. R. Nickson, "The Itaipu Hydro-Electric Project", in *Bulletin of Latin American Research* (U.K.: October 1982), p. 5.

20. R.P. Misra and N. Dung, "Large cities: Growth Dynamics and Emerging Problems", in *Habitat International* (Vol. 7, No. 5/6, 1983).

21. S. Schwartzman, *Sao Paulo e o Estado Nacional* (Sao Paulo: Difel, 1975).

22. "The Morning After" in *The Economist*, 12/3/1983.

23. See *World Development Report* (New York: Oxford University Press, 1988), pp. 154–167.

3

The Administration of
Social Resources at
State and Local Levels

The Housing Market in Greater Sao Paulo

This chapter is mainly concerned with the analysis of the public housing agencies in Greater Sao Paulo. However a better understanding of the place and function of these agencies requires a comparative description of the state of Sao Paulo within the Brazilian context. The state of Sao Paulo is roughly the size of the UK and with 25 million inhabitants in 1985, it has about half of the population of the UK. Sao Paulo is undoubtedly the main centre of economic activity, and the richest state within Brazil. The taxation base originating from industrialization made the state of Sao Paulo's government one of the most important public budgets in the country. Income per head is more than double that of the rest of the country's states, and it is considered as Brazil's industrial powerhouse. As a consequence of its public investment capacity, Sao Paulo has the largest availability of transport, communication, electric power and urban infrastructure of the Brazilian states. Put together, these factors explain the increasing attractiveness of Sao Paulo as an area of destination for internal migration. The latter is characterized by a great imbalance in distribution of population and economic activity: the metropolitan area shows higher density and larger economic activity than the agrarian parts of the state. Greater Sao Paulo had a population of 12.3 million in 1980 and a projected growth rate of 4.4 percent thus ranking it as the fifth largest metropolis in the world.

The state of Sao Paulo is located in the southeast region of Brazil, has an area of 247.898 square Km, and a total population of 25 million inhabitants. It is also the most urbanized among the Brazilian states. In 1970, the population living in urban settlements reached 80 percent of the state's total population (67 percent if the GSP area is excluded), whereas this proportion for the country as a whole was 56 percent. The economic growth is strongly concentrated in the metropolitan centre and in a few medium size cities (such as Santos; Campinas; Ribeiro Preto; Sao Jose de Campos and Sorocaba). The contribution of the state of Sao Paulo to the formation of the Brazilian GDP reached 39 percent in 1970 and was increased by the end of 1980. The high speed of growth of the state's GDP—4.8 percent average annual rate—had made it possible for Sao Paulo to maintain its per capita income at twice the national average. The taxation power attributed to the Brazilian state is regulated by federal law. The tax revenues are, at the end, determined by the performance of the economic activities located within each state. Sao Paulo's revenue equals to 60 percent of the corresponding item in the Federal Government's budget. That is, Sao Paulo's budget shows a tax revenue that is 48 percent of that of the other 25 Brazilian states added together. These facts rank the state of Sao Paulo's budget in the second place of importance within the Brazilian governmental structure.

Put another way, the government of Sao Paulo is the second most important agent of public expenditure in the country. The state budget for 1984 was revealed by the state secretary of planning, Jose Serra, to be approximately Cr$5 trillion and 400 billions (equivalent to US $5.4 billion). Bearing in mind that Sao Paulo is the main area of origin of tax revenues for the federal government, it places Sao Paulo as the most important state in the federal structure, as far as policy making and implementation are concerned.

To understand better the political and economic role played by Sao Paulo, in the context of the federal government, one has to go back as early as the 19th century, when coffee appeared as the main crop in the country's economy becoming an agricultural-based settlement through which the province of Sao Paulo started to acquire its hegemony.[1] During this period Sao Paulo's importance in the political sphere was clearer than during any other time. Its economic and political interests were advanced through monetary and exchange policies, guaranteeing foreign loans to the state of Sao Paulo, influencing tax, immigration laws and the distribution of revenues in a way to benefit the state as much as possible. The political power enjoyed by the state of Sao Paulo shifted to the federal government and its new allies, during the Vargas era. The turning point was the abortive attempt to topple Vargas in 1932. The armed revolt of 1932 was the last step in the long period of discontent and confrontation between the central government and the most important state in the federation, marking the actual end of what was considered the "Old Republic".[2]

During the period of 1945–64 the political role and potential importance of Sao Paulo were considerably undermined by the key aspects of the electoral process and the political systems giving significant importance to a process of "territorial accommodation". Sao Paulo being one of the main forces of the process of industrialization, urbanization and economic growth, and at the same time being "underrepresented" both in Congress and in the federal executive, is one of the great political paradoxes. Strengthening the powers of the centre over the states was meant to keep the economic growth and its implications, under federal control, and to maintain in check the growing process of politicization. The period following 1964 saw changes in the balance of power—financial and industrial bourgeoisie assumed political power allying themselves with the military and civil bureaucracy.

Today there are clear attempts at making moves towards overall administrative reform supporting the process creating decentralized agencies aiming at making possible the development of a "productivity role", trying to move towards relative autonomy of some decentralized agencies and to minimize the effect of the generalized process of institutional power concentration at the federal level.[3]

Together with the increasing economic activity in this state it is possible to see significant changes in the political struggle for power at local levels of government. What we may be witnessing in the "Paulista" housing market, is the increased control of the government party (PDS) over the vast resources which state and city governments are called upon to provide. Both local and national politicians (e.g., Maluf and Andreazza) decide on the level of public housing provision, on the "mix of tenures", the location of municipal and state housing schemes, the kind of welfare and other services provided in these areas and the allocation of tenants to these housing schemes. State and municipal housing agencies' lack of financial resources, for revenue, has been systematically denied. For anything of significance to be constructed by the state, and especially by the municipality, requires intercession with the federal government, where resources of all kinds are concentrated. The only other source of finance is to seek funds from international lending institutions like the World Bank (see chapter 2).

With the establishment of the BNH in 1964, a specific financing agency was founded for each of the different segments of the housing market which was defined by the BNH. The "popular market" that was initially limited to low income people where family income must be in the range of less or equal to three minimum monthly salaries and later on broadened to a range of five minimum salaries, would be serviced by "Housing Agencies" (COHABs)—either state or municipal. The so called "economic market" initially entrusted to construct housing units for a population with a family income in the range of three to six minimum monthly wages, a limit later on extended, would be serviced by housing cooperatives composed basically of professional categories. The "cooperatives" contract work and select applicants according to general guidelines established by the BNH. After the houses have been marketed the "cooperatives" cease to exist; they are constructed by INOCOOP, a cooperative housing agency created in 1964 as part of the military government's strategy of controlling the previous powerful trade unions.

CODESPAULO, the development corporation of Sao Paulo constructs popular housing for people with an income range of up to five minimum monthly wages. It also participates with other public and private agencies in programs of slum eradication.

The SBPE (Brazilian Saving and Loan System) embraces the second main group of BNH agents, those specialising in middle and upper income housing. The SBPE comprises three main sets of institutions: the privately owned, joint-stock Real Estate Credit Companies (Sociedades de Credito Imobilario, SCI); the mutualist Savings and Loan Associations (Associacoes de Poupanca e Emprestimo, APE) and the Federal and State Savings Banks (Caixas Economicas, CE). The SBPE is supervised and controlled by the BNH which approves the opening of new branches and establishes interest rates, reserve requirements and other financial norms.[4]

Greater Sao Paulo, the dynamic center of the richest state in the country, has an enormous housing deficit. With a population of almost 13 million, containing 50 percent of the entire state's population and with new migrants arriving at a rate of 1000 per day, it was estimated in 1980 that the city had a deficit of 800,000 housing units needed to shelter about 4.5 million inhabitants. In his research on the evolution of Sao Paulo's slums (favelas), Camargo analyses the increase of the favela population.[5] The total number of favelados rose to 1.2 million in 1982. In 1972 to 1978 the slum population increased by 350 percent and from 1978 to 1982 by 950 percent. Thus in ten years there was an accumulated increase of 1300 percent. While the median increase of slum dwellers was 31 percent per year the total population increased at a rate of 5.5 percent. The 72 percent of the Brazilian workforce earning less than two minimum monthly salaries are obviously outside the Housing Finance System (SFH). GSP with an annual increase of 600,000 inhabitants per year, which is equivalent to an annual demand of 120,000 new housing units per year, has supplied its population with only 160,000 units since 1964 (the latter figure includes INOCOOP,

TABLE 3.1   Construction Position of the Public Housing Agencies in
            Greater Sao Paulo

	COHAB/SP Until 1979	CODESPAULO Until 1980	INOCOOP/SP Until 1982
Total Units	90.000	34.000	30.347
Average Cost (In UPC)*	800	354	1750
Average Income of Buyers (Minimum Salaries)	4	5.5	6.6

* UPC: Standard Capital Unit - constant value for financial indexation

COHAB and CODESPAULO housing units until 1980) most of which
were not attainable by the low income sectors.

Administrating Social Resources at Local Levels

The COHABs are the promoting agents of the BNH for the "popular
market". Initially the market tried to attend to families with a range
of one to three minimum salaries but later on it was amplified to a
limit of five minimum salaries. COHABs are joint-stock companies,
but at least 51 percent of their shares must be owned by state or
municipal authorities. The bulk of their operations are directed towards
providing housing for low income families with at least three minimum
salaries (see Table 3.1). The cost of each housing unit was generally to
be less than 320 UPC but this was amplified to—800 UPC (equivalent
to US $6200 in December 1983). The COHABs are controlled by the
public sector and the disinterest of the private sector in participating
is an indicator of the lack of attraction to the popular housing market.
The general programs of the COHABs, as well as the specific construction projects have to be approved by the BNH. It is the COHABS'
responsibility or the states' or municipalities' to implement the completion of parts of the projects that are perhaps not financed by the
BNH. The resources used for financing originate from the "Fundo de
Garantia por Tempo de Servico" (FGTS)—a system of social insurance
which requires compulsory contributions by employed people—of which
the BNH is the administrator. At present the length of finance for the
popular market is up to 25 years with relatively low rates of interest
(approximately 1 percent to 3 percent). Annually, 60 days after the

increase of the minimum salary, there is a monetary correction of the loans, in accordance with indexes defined by the federal government.

In the projects administered by the COHAB, the local municipalities nearly always are in charge of the urbanization of the land, the extension of the roads and of the water and sewage systems. In some cases, the local authorities also participate in donating land and in other cases the COHAB itself purchases at market prices. What is important, is that computing all the costs and taxes of administration, the cost of a residential unit can not exceed 500 UPC's (Standard Capital Unit— whose value is adjusted each quarter in line with the monthly revaluations of the ORTN. At the beginning of each quarter the value of one UPC is the value of ORTN. In July 1975, this was Cr$119—about US $14 at the official exchange rate, or about US $12 at the black market rate.)

During the years 1967/1970 COHABs (as a whole) were receiving 44 percent of all of the BNH's housing funds. Between 1970 and 1976 the bank diverted a large proportion of its housing funds to the guarantee of SBPE agents' loans and to credit for housing materials purchase by higher income groups. Indeed the only program which really applied to the majority of the population with a family income of less than five minimum salaries, that run by the state and municipal COHABs, saw its funds cut seriously during this period. In 1975 it received only three per cent of total BNH funds and six per cent of housing funds.[6]

One of the consequences of the severe cuts in BNH financial support during this period was that state and municipal housing agencies began to look for new sources of finance. International organizations such as the World Bank, USAID and BIRD, were approached by COHABs based in large urban centers. These organisations not only financed urbanization projects but also urban and housing plans.

In 1978, the World Bank approved the finance of US $92 million for the construction of housing units, destinated for a population with an income of up to 3 minimum salaries in Pernambuco, Bahia and Sao Paulo. The COHAB will construct 20,000 "embrioes" (small houses built for ex-favelados) and "urbanized plots", the majority in the eastern zone of S.P., to attend a population that until today is marginalized by the BNH housing programs.[7]

The median cost of the units should be inferior to 350 UPC. The main difference between finance by an international organization to that by the BNH is that the COHAB has to follow rigid restrictions in the contract especially in relation to construction time and on imposed

limitations on the income levels of the inhabitants (up to three minimum salaries). The National Housing Bank was the major source of
finance. In September 1976 it (BNH) loaned the equivalent of US $80
million to sustain the works for three months until the end of the year.
By comparison, its budget for "social interest" (PLANHAP) housing
in the entire country was less than US $130 million for the whole
year.[8] The Sao Paulo municipality not only received the loans and
finance and transferred the resources to the Metro Company but was
also responsible for the repayment of debts. By August 1976 the municipality had committed capital of approximately US $460 million.[9]

Until the mid-1970s, COHAB/SP had constructed less than 4000
housing units, as not only the municipality but also the BNH invested
in mass transport systems (such as the Metro in S.P.) and in urban
infrastructure. With an imposed limit of financing housing up to a cost
of 320 UPC (Standard Capital Unit—a constant value for financial
indexation), the municipal housing company could not feasably produce
large scale low income housing. Only at the end of 1979 did the BNH
raise the limit to a more feasible limit of 800 UPC enabling large scale
construction. During the administration of Paulo Egydio Martin's government in the period 1975/79 private construction firms began to be
interested in investing in low income housing as the middle sector
market became saturated. Another factor which contributed to this
"downward" move was the BNH's change of policy that increased the
UPC limit to 800 (in large metropolitan centers such as Rio de Janeiro
and Sao Paulo). During the Geisel government, 1974/1979, high rates
of inflation began to appear. These rates were partially fed by the
index-linking system that had been built into the economy since the
mid-1960s. Since only official credit instruments were indexed, savings
"fled" to the index-linked sector.[10] The BNH which is the administrator
of the "Social Security for Employees" (FGTS), an index linked fund,
became during this period Brazil's second largest bank with assets of
over US $1000 million. The enormous growth of the FGTS, which
remained through all this period the most important element of BNH's
resources, allowed it to invest in housing through its agents—mainly
the 34 COHABs that are dispersed throughout the whole country—and
increase the UPC limit to 800.

The construction industry faced a dilemma—either cut down drastically their workforce or reduce their profit margins and construct low
cost public housing.[11] The partial reaction to this dilemma was to
introduce new construction techniques that were capital intensive (as
opposed to previously labor intensive traditional methods) and build
large numbers of units.[12] During this period a substantial number of
construction firms collapsed. In spite of the apparent security built into

the public housing system more than half of the COHAB's clients have delays in the mortgage payment. This is basically because of a loss of income and by the tendency of wealth concentration in Brazil.[13] (A study by the IBGE foundation revealed that the income of laborers with one to five salaries was reduced from 66 percent of the total Brazilian income in 1970, to 45 percent in 1976). In Sao Paulo the indice of arrears by purchasers was 46 percent in 1978, while in the Southern region it reached 57 percent attaining a level of 77 percent in Rio de Janeiro. Sao Paulo's COHAB, which has the "lion share" of BNH funding (for state housing) has one of the lowest rates of arrear payments—10.5 percent—according to Bueno de Miranda (regional director of the BNH in Sao Paulo).[14]

The matter of non payment is of crucial importance to the effectiveness and philosophy not only of COHAB but also of the entire structure of the housing finance system, even if the system can support some non-payment, it has become so central to its operating principles that no open subsidies are offered.[15] Not only are COHAB officials anxious to improve the levels of mortgage repayment but also the BNH whose president declared in 1983 that 720,000 inhabitants were overdue in their mortgage payments out of a total of 4 million mortgagees. The federal government's salary policy, since 1979, has been to reduce the workers' income—mainly that of the middle sectors. This has resulted in a "threat" to the Federal Housing System (SFH) as salaries should accompany the loans, guaranteeing the ideal relation between mortgages and wages. A political mobilization for the "boycott" of the mortgages was initiated in the whole of Brazil as a reaction to the BNH's increase of the mortgage payment readjustment—whereas salaries were only readjusted at a rate of 80 percent of the inflation index, mortgages were readjusted at a rate of 100 percent. Opposition politicians, such as deputy Freito Nobres leader of the PMDB and deputy Djalma Bom of the PT, participated in the mortgagees movements and appealed for a "boycott" of mortgage payments to the bank believing that if hundreds of thousands do not pay on schedule their loans the BNH will have to reduce the readjustment of 130 percent that was introduced in July 1983.

The total number of housing units financed by the COHABs in 1978 was slightly more than 250,000, distributed in the following way: Rio de Janeiro (18 percent); Sao Paulo (15 percent); Minas Gerais and Espirito Santo (7 percent); Federal District (10 percent); North-East region (28 percent); Northern region, Mato Grosso and Goias (10 percent). These figures are misleading if taken in the nominal value. Although according to the latter more units were constructed in Rio de Janeiro than elsewhere, Sao Paulo's COHAB has the "lion share" of

BNH funding (for state housing). While presiding a ceremony in Tau-
bate, Mario Andreazza (Minister of the Interior) announced that the
state of Sao Paulo would receive this year from the BNH—US $1.71
billion; out of this US $1 billion was allocated for housing; basic
sanitation (US $698 million) and urban development—US $12 million.[16]
Andreazza explained that more than half of the Bank's budget would
be allocated to Sao Paulo, as it is one of the most needy states of the
union. He stressed that the resources for Sao Paulo were nearly double
the amount of the previous year's global budget. Although Andreazza
declared that the BNH would allocate more than half of its resources
to the federal union's neediest state (Sao Paulo), the South-East region
as a whole received 48 percent of the Bank's resources (as of 31/12/
82).[17]

Sao Paulo state was allocated only 27 percent of the total with
COHAB/SP receiving 12 percent and CODESPAULO a mere 3 percent.
The reduction in the transfer of BNH resources to the South-East
indicates a changing trend of investing more in urban development in
the pro-government North East states. With Sao Paulo as well as Rio
de Janeiro and Minas Gerais, Brazil's largest urban centers, electing
opposition state governments (PMDB and PT) in 1982, the federal
government under the leadership of Mario Andreazza (Minister of
Interior) diverted substantial BNH funds away from the industrialized
South East towards the "development" of the North East. Distortions
in the distribution of financial resources resulted in the deterioration
of the housing market in Sao Paulo. Not only were funds diverted to
the North East but they were also utilized to help cover the federal
public sector deficit (see chapter 2). The money of the FGTS and the
vast deposits in the saving accounts, are not used, like in the past,
only for housing but are being mobilized to finance public expenditure
debits.[18]

Toward New Forms of State Housing Provision

Since 1975, under the new administration coordinated by Bourroul—
the COHAB's President—the metropolitan housing company of S.P.
constructed nearly 94,000 new units that were allotted in fourteen
different projects, housing in 1984 a population of approximately half
a million inhabitants (see Table 3.2). Jose Celestino Bourroul was
appointed by the prefecture. As COHAB/SP is an organization whose
capital is largely owned by the municipality, the appointment of the
directorship is subject to the prefect's decision who can also select
subordinate staff. The majority of the projects were concentrated in the
eastern zone of the city and two were situated in the extreme western

TABLE 3.2 General Balance of Achieved Results by Cohab S.P. 1965–1979

HOUSING UNITS DESCRIPTION	HOUSES	FLATS	PLOTS	TOTAL
Delivered Until 1975				3579
Delivered Until 31.3.79				
Guaianazes		1000		1000
Borore	1233	518		1751
Carapicuiba	856	3412		4268
Itaquera 1	650	3260		3910
Itaquera 2/3	1013	990		2003
Self Help	1071			1071
Sub-Total	5825	8180		14003
In Construction				
Parque IPE	2	198		200
Sapopemba	23	176		199
Itaquera 1		8060		8060
Itaquera 2/3	950	9440		10390
Borore		816		816
Carapicuiba		2676		2676
Guaianazes		260		260
Elisio Leite		2920		2920
Self Help	777			777
Sub-Total	1752	24546		26298
In Selling Phase				
Guarulhos	128			128
Itaquera 1		950		950
Itaquera 2/3	2459	5370		7829
Jardim Sao Paulo	110	530	259	899
Sub-Total	2697	6850	259	9806
Project Contracted with the BNH & Being Accomplished				
Jardim S.P.	1044	3440	665	5352
S. Etelvina	6636	5570	6105	18311
Carapicuiba		5888		5888
Itapevi	2735	2352	1782	6869
Sub-Total	10415	17250	8755	36420
Total	20689	56826	9014	90124

Source: COHAB S.P., April 1979

zone. Together these projects house an estimated 115,000 tenants in 21,116 units. The smaller projects were situated in the Northern and Southern zones of the metropolitan. Sao Paulo in the last decade, has followed zoning patterns similar to those of other third world metropolitans—that is:

> The poor are forced to move to areas a long way from the main areas of employment; long bus journeys are therefore becoming commonplace, which poses an important time and economic constraint on family life.[19]

The major achievement of the Bourroul administration was not only the construction of large numbers of housing units but also the building up of an immense land reserve—9 million square meters of empty land and a total of 32 million square meters of houses either already built or being executed—that was financed by the BNH (see chapter 4). In 1983, COHAB's presidency was assumed by Raymundo de Paschoal who declared that the new municipal and state government's housing policies would be implemented immediately. As a consequence of an oppositon administration being elected in the state of Sao Paulo, BNH financial transfers to the COHAB were reduced drastically. The municipal housing agency, as of 1982, has hardly invested in new projects but concentrated in selling and finishing units built by the previous administration. The new directory of the COHAB does not yet have a complete evaluation of the housing projects, constructed by the previous administrations. Meanwhile only general lines of intention have been planned—construction of smaller projects, nearer to the urbanized areas of the city that are already integrated with the city.[20] Raymundo de Paschoal, COHAB's president, intends to convince civil construction entrepreneurs to offer their product to a population with an income range of 1 to 3 s.m., the same as COHAB's.[21] Under the new "philosophy", only small to medium sized ones will be constructed nearer to the urbanized areas. One of the COHAB's ways of constructing, without a change of the BNH's finance policy, is not to purchase land in expensive areas of the city but to exchange COHAB land with the private sector (the COHAB has an enormous land reserve of which 80 percent is concentrated in the eastern zone of the city). But Paschoal is not too optimistic about the outcomes of COHAB's new policies: If we do not have alternative ways to renegotiate the land, we will continue to invest only in the eastern zone.[22]

Administrating Social Resources at State Levels

In most of the states of Brazil, there are COHABs which act as housing companies with a state-wide responsibility. Sao Paulo State has preserved its own State housing company (CODESPAULO formerly CECAP), limiting the BNH inspired COHABs to a municipal level of responsibilty.[23] CECAP, (Caixa Estadual de Casas para o Povo) was one of the first state housing companies to be created in Brazil. On the 10th of October 1949 this new housing agency was formed with the following objectives:

1. As an autonomous housing company CECAP would have a State-wide responsibility.
2. To finance the construction of or construct in its own plots (or those donated by the State or Municipality) popular housing either for sale or renting.
3. To give credit to public entities who desire to construct residential housing for their employees.
4. The rent charged could not be higher than 8 percent of the total value of the house.
5. Interest charged on loans would have a ceiling of 12 percent p.a. for a period of up to 20 years.
6. The CECAP would be administered by a Superintendent and by a Fiscal Council, both nominated by the State Governor.

CECAP would be subordinate to the State Secretary for Labor, Industry and Commerce and would consequently plan working class housing and residential projects near industrial areas.[24] The "Paulista" Governor during this era (1947–50) was Adehmar P. De Barros who campaigned on the slogan "He steals but gets things done". Adhemar, who ran a patronage machine, anticipated the need for a charismatic image and posed as a man of the people of Sao Paulo. Transport policy was the main concern of this state governor. In the Capital it was highly commended that it was necessary to expand urban services to the new peripheries, and also the issue of the housing problem of the lower sectors was perceived.[25]

Due to the rapid population growth in GSP and various related problems the government began to recognize the importance of social policy dimensions. GSP had an average yearly growth rate of 6 percent during the post WWII period. In 1951 Lucas Nogueira Garcez succeeded Barros as Governor. A change of policies stemmed from a belief that "industrial decentralization" would bring forth a rapid economic development. CECAP began during that epoch (1951–54) to construct in industrial areas in the interior of the state as the government began to develop infrastructural services that could be characterized as "urban". Among the latter electric energy and sanitation were emphasized. It was only with the re-election of Adhemar de Barros to state governorship in 1963 that the State Secretary for Labor, Industry and Commerce emphasized the development of housing projects. A return to planning popular housing estates resulted in pointing out the importance of CECAP as the Secretary carried out research on the industrial labor force in Sao Paulo and also studies on the economic development of cities in the Interior with more than 100,000 inhabitants. The latter became the principal agency which linked state policy with federal. Thus the Secretary for Labor, Industry and Commerce did not restrict itself to the economic sector but extended to other areas such as the "desfavelamento" program.

Until the mid 1970s, CECAP had constructed only ten thousand housing units. Paulo Egydio Martins' state government (1975–77) reactivated the public housing market. The transformation of CECAP (a public agency subordinated to the Secretary of Industry) into a society of mixed-economy resulted from studies carried out before Paulo Egydio became state governor.[26]

A public agency that specialized in planning—PLANASA—was contracted to survey the housing demands and project future patterns. The projected deficit in this sector was estimated at one million units up to 1980. The basic characteristic of the government (Paulo Egydio Martins), was the emphasis on development. The concept of development did not relate only to economic growth, but also in the process of integrating the individual in society, on improvement in the quality of life.[27] Fundamental values considered by this government were the reduction of social inequalities and in the cost of basic services for the benefit of the lower income population. In the area of housing, Martins declared that it is necessary to create an adequate system so that the population would have access to housing. This would be done by stimulating CECAP's activities, whose namesake was changed from "Caixa Estadual de Casas para o Povo" to "Companhia Estadual de Casas para o Povo"; the housing agencies would be reformed so that they would have an adequate capacity to execute government strategy; reduce the housing deficit; improve the existing units; increase the supply of units and reduce production costs.[28]

During this period the Itaquera project began.[29] The housing problem that was perceived as an important issue in thirty years of governments, did not receive the same treatment in the creation of administrative mechanisms. Only the government of Adhemar de Barros, between 1947–50, intervened directly in this issue, creating the CECAP and elaborating Popular Housing Plans. The housing of lower income sectors and of public servants was an objective of innumerable plans, projects and studies of the governments of Adhemar (1947), Garcez (1951–54) and Janio Quadros (1955–58). During Carvalho Pinto's governorship

(1959–62), there appears to have been an interest in this public issue only in relation to unionized laborers. From the Abreu Sodre government (1967–70) onwards, public housing projects surged, like Cumbica as well as in the interior of the state (during Laudo Natel's government). Paulo Egydio Martins gave priority in the popular housing sector to the large urban centers, elaborating self-help projects directed by CECAP. The public housing works carried out during the period 1947–77 and mainly financed by IPESP and by CECAP, were mostly housing estates.

Coping with Political Corruption

In this book political corruption is defined as the illicit use of public agencies' material and jurisdictional resources, the violation of agency rules and procedures, or the functionaries failure to follow official directives for their own personal gain. This study suggests that bureaucrats and politicians (individually and in groups) who cannot obtain positions which allow them to influence decision-making seek to unseat those in power. As government takes on more and more functions, particularly in regulating and managing the economy, the number of potentially lucrative and powerful positions greatly increases, quite beyond a mere handful of cabinet posts and electoral offices. Countless boards, commissions and government corporations must be manned. Successful political leaders (e.g., Paulo Maluf) devote considerable ingenuity and resources to rewarding the faithful and attempting to withhold advantages from those who oppose them. The proliferation of public enterprises, with some governmental authority over the allocation and use of economic resources, provides political parties (e.g., the PDS) with means of inducing political conformity, as contracts may go only to the party faithful as a reward for political support.

During the mid-1970s, a series of public enquiries were carried out on the expenditure and distribution policies of CECAP. The acquisition of land by the latter, which has one of the largest reserves in the whole state of S.P. (nearly 3 million square metres), was not always purchased at market prices. CECAP would spend more than Cr$20 million in purchasing an area of 1.07 million square meters (near Bauru—a city in the interior of S.P.), when in the city there were 370,000 square meters of land belonging to the state.[30] Another accusation by the Brazilian Press was that CECAP purchased a large plot in the city of Rio Claro twenty days before the local elections and the inscriptions for the purchase of of public housing were carried out in the residence of Alvaro Perin, President of the local ARENA party, who was also the lawyer of the ex-landowner.[31] Perin was a candidate for the mayorship of Rio Claro and in the past had lost the elections to other members of his party. During the inscription of candidates the campaign for mayorship intensified. The latter ARENA candidate was known to have had political connections with the State Secretary of the Interior, Raphael Baldacci, who later on threatened to sue the Journal do Brasil which had published reports on CECAP's irregularities in land acquisition policies. An inquiry commission into the acquisition of land by the former housing agency was brought forward by the municipality of Rio Claro. A month later the governor Paulo Egydio told the "Arenista" state leadership that the party supports the intiative of MDB to constitute a special inquiry commission (CEI) to analyze the accounts of CECAP.[32]

Deputy Baldacci, by amplifying the portfolio of the Secretary of Interior, became one of the most influential politicians in S.P. state. With the accessibility of two eminently political public enterprises, CECAP and SUDELPA, he consolidated and multiplied the basis for support in hundreds of Paulista municipalities. To implement this scheme, Baldacci contradicted many times the political interests of other "Arenistas", who later took advantage of the denouncing of corruption to try and demoralize and dilute his electoral power (he was the Federal deputy most voted by the "Arenistas", surpassing even Adhemar de Barros Filho). Several prominent "Arenistas" tried to convince the state governor, Egydio, to remove Baldacci from the government to preserve a self-image of austerity. There could have been a reason for their lack of success: his Secretary of Interior is an element well related to the Chief of the "Casa Civil da Presidencia da Republica", General Golbery do Couto e Silva, whom he knew since the Janio Quadro government.[33]

On March 1977, the Special Inquiry Commission (CEI) questioned the political behaviour of Baldacci in regard to his involvement in public housing distribution during a period of elections with more than 3000 candidates in Rio Claro inscribing for the new CECAP project. According to the opposition party, MDB, a state secretary should not intervene in favour of his party during a political campaign.[34] A few days later the President of CECAP, Juvenal Juvencio, announced his resignation claiming that CECAP was a political organ whose administration efficiency reflects the image of the state government and the secretary of Interior. When interviewed by journalists the former President did not deny that he was politically linked to Baldacci. The newly appointed president of this housing organization, Ismael Armond, declared that CECAP would have economic difficulties as the previous administration left behind a deficit of Cr$50 million. A new planning and administrative strategy was initiated because of a lack of previous planning. Some of the projects being constructed in more than 60 municipalities in S.P. state were not even marketable because of the lack of transport and other basic public services. According to the new strategy, 22,000 housing units and 21,000 "urbanized plots", would be initiated with BNH finance.

In explaining the new policy, Armond declared that CECAP cannot construct what is not possible to sell. For this agency to be commercially viable, the company president declared that of 70 cities, only in 20 would construction be carried out. It is obvious that the previous administration had constructed and planned not according to economic or social sense but conforming to the political ambitions of Raphael Baldacci—the State Secretary of the Interior. Although the latter aspired to become governor of Sao Paulo, the ARENA party nominated Paulo Maluf as designate for this key position. Baldacci succeeded eventually to be elected to the Senate.

The state government stopped the construction of 5000 popular housing units of the 20,000 units foreseen in the first stage of the 1977 State Housing Plan. The motive behind this, was that CECAP, whose main objective was to construct low-income housing for a population with up to 5 minimum salaries, gave priority to luxury apartments, consuming most of its resources. An example of this distortion was the Araraquara housing complex, with a swimming pool and other luxury facilities, but with a price of nearly Cr$1 million, it did not find buyers. The new administration, under the directorship of Armond, tried to correct inherited errors and at the same time attempted to achieve the aims of the housing plans. During the years 1977/79, according to Armond's declarations, 160,000 units destined exclusively for a population of 5 minimum salaries would be constructed. In order to achieve these ambitious goals, several administrative and operative changes would be carried out. Priority to low income housing and increases in the use of state and federal funds and BNH financing were the fundamental changes. At the same time Armond wanted to avoid the transformation of the housing agency into a large public enterprise with huge administrative expenses. A unique way to achieve this was to create a new type of bidding system. Construction firms from now onwards would become responsible for all the stages of housing projects. Thus, CECAP transferred all the problems of direct involvement to the construction process. Even the function of purchasing land would be a responsibility of the private sector building firms. In areas where CECAP already had a large reserve of land (e.g., Barretos, Indaiatuba, Rio Claro), this new construction system would not be implemented. Of the 20,000 units that were to be built, 8000 to 12,000 low income units would be in the metropolitan region.

Even though the new administration had committed itself not to purchase lands directly as a consequence of previous public enquiries, on July 1978 CECAP again purchased 11 acres in Villa Jardim (Botucatu), with the intention of constructing popular housing units. CECAP bought each acre for a sum which was equal to twice the value of properties outside the urban centre. More than double the amount of the purchase price was paid not to the land owner, but to the intermediary—Mayr Godoy. The latter was a Paulista lawyer well known for his political connections, having defended Laudo Natel in the judicial appeal by which the ex-governor intended to oppose the nomination of Paulo Maluf as Egydio's successor in the ARENA convention. CECAP paid Godoy Cr$700,000 per acre, a price considered as one of the highest ever paid, while the land owner received only Cr$ 250,000 per acre.

The administration of state public enterprises is subject to changes with the election of a new government. Thus, with the election of Sao Paulo's governor—Paulo Maluf, in February 1979, a new president for CECAP was nominated—Oscar Klabin Segal. With the change of administration at CECAP, policy changes were brought forward by Segal. He intended to reduce the agency's huge deficit by selling housing lots at a loss, some of which had been vacant since 1976. With the financial help of the BNH, which promised loans of up to Cr$10 billion, housing would be constructed in GSP. This formed part of the overall housing program of the Figueiredo government which intended to construct six million units in the next six years. In a meeting with the Minister of Interior, Mario Andreazza, the president of CECAP, presented a construction plan of one million popular housing units to be built in the whole of S.P. state in the next few years. This program destined for families with 1.5 to 5 minimum salaries, intruded into the COHAB housing market. Oscar Klabin Segal, the administrator, architect and politician who was nominated president of this housing agency in 1979, resigned a year later after being heavily pressured by Maluf whom he accused of being interested in creating a "social turmoil". He identified the governor with the group inside the party (PDS), that desired an authoritarian regime and political endurement.[35]

The reason for Klabin's resignation was linked with the nomination of Jose Oswaldo Muller da Silva—the son of an advisor to the state tribunal for accounts—to the post of administrative director of this public agency. In a special assembly of directors (although the summon had been denounced by Klabin) the new director was elected after heavy pressures from Maluf who appointed him officially. According to Klabin there was a mutual agreement with the governor. Having been nominated to the presidency of CECAP the latter would have the liberty to choose the directors of the enterprise and make public irregular events. It was in these terms that he accepted the position after a long conversation with the governor, whom he had helped to elect in the ARENA convention. Klabin declared that he had nothing personal against the new director but considered it unethical that the son of a counsellor of the Tribunal of Accounts, would manipulate the accounts that this Tribunal would investigate.[36]

Previously, the CECAP assembly had authorized its director to make public land purchase irregularities that had occurred during Paulo Egydio Martins government, but Maluf pressurized him violently not to disclose the latter as he claimed to have a political agreement with the ex-governor not to reveal past affairs. Martins, later on, denounced the existence of such an agreement with Maluf: the excuse of an agreement is simply ludicrous.[37] A short period after the realization of the itinerant government in Santo Andre, Klabin had another misunderstanding with Maluf who had promised the city's inhabitants to construct 45,000 houses. I confirmed the promise (Klabin), but he (Maluf) refused to finance the project because the mayor of S.Andre, Lincoln Grillo, did not join the PDS. The project should have benefitted 45,000 favelados.[38] The insensitivity of the governor towards a social program, led me to believe that he wanted to create a social turmoil and does not want to cooperate with President Figueiredo.[39]

Maluf appointed Elias Correa de Camargo as the new president of CECAP after the resignation of Klabin. Camargo was "famous" in his previous positions at CEAGESP and at INOCOOP S.P. He was dismissed from the presidency of the two public agencies by governor Abreu Sodre and by the BNH. The dismissal from CEAGESP (previously CEASA) was related to the governor of S.P. finding out that Camargo had travelled in Europe for two months at CECAP's expense. Later on, while directing INOCOOP S.P, he was responsible for large financial losses to the BNH. The bank which financed INOCOOP projects forced his dismissal after he had constructed luxury apartments in areas planned for low income housing. With his nomination as president of CECAP, Camargo would again be responsible for the allocation of BNH resources. Camargo, who was known to belong to the Maluf group, manoeuvred politically in a way that would meet the objectives of the governor and not those of CECAP. Maluf surrounded himself with elements that supported his policies and was not interested in the (administrative) capabilities of his nominees.[40] The BNH's lack of approval toward the nomination of the new president created difficulties in the financing of housing projects in S.P. During the Camargo administration a relatively low number of new projects were constructed (see Figure 3.1).

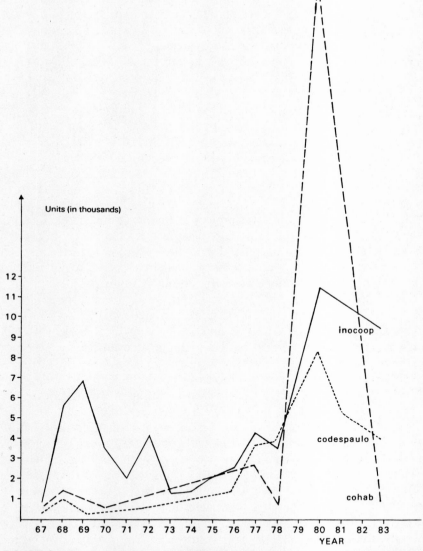

FIGURE 3.1 Trends in Public Housing Construction in Greater Sao Paulo, 1967–83.
Source: compiled by the author.

The Consequences of Reorganizing a Bureaucracy

One important power granted to political executives is the power to reorganize bureaucracies. This power is not totally executive, with legislatures having at times equal powers. So a politician like Paulo Maluf was able to effect extensive reorganizations and use those reorganizations for his own purposes in office. The tradition of creating new agencies and promoting established employees allowed the new Maluf state government to build important political support. Friends and supporters were brought into newly created positions of prestige and power. Surely, the newly promoted bureaucrats were aware of their benefactor and recognized the necessity for reciprocation. Consequently, while some waste was involved, new agencies certainly pay handsome short-term political dividends (e.g., Maluf's nomination as a Presidential candidate). On January 1981, the State Secretary of Industry, Commerce, Science and Technology announced the foundation of a "Development Corporation of Sao Paulo" (CODESPAULO) which would replace CE-CAP. The latter's functions of constructing popular housing would be continued and in addition would analyse the municipalities' industrial policies and if necessary initiate the implementation of industrial projects. A consultation service would be provided to industries that planned to integrate the provision of housing for their labor force within their premises. Several of this new agency's functions were actually concurrent with those of the State Planning Agency (EMPLASA) which is linked to the Secretary for Metropolitan Affairs. The Secretary responsible for CODESPAULO affirmed that this agency would not obstruct but complement EMPLASA's activities by carrying out research on industrial development. However according to EMPLASA planners a study was already completed by the Coordinating Department of the State Secretary for Industry and Commerce.[41]

The idea of investing in urban infrastructure to develop industrial estates was not new and was probably inspired by experiences carried out during the first half of this century in Villa Maria Velha and Flacacao Indiana where laborers lived in the factory premises. As CODESPAULO did not have legal powers to try and achieve industrial decentralization it would use, according to its President, Camargo, a tactic of persuasion—they would obtain finance and the necessary infrastructure for a badly situated industry in Santo Andre if it would transfer its premises to Tiete.[42] In addition, participation in the finance and construction of housing for the industry's workforce would be offered at the new site. Paulo Maluf dismantled CECAP with the pretext that its work conflicted with that of the "state building society" (Caixa Economica Federal).[43] According to Camargo what was necessary were only a few administrative amendments. As Mayor of Sao Paulo and later as governor of the state, Maluf built up not only a solid base of support among the figures of the political and military establishment most closely identified with the regime which had ruled Brazil over the last 20 years, but he also tried to attract the support of business and industry by promising unstinting support for private enterprises.

> During 1979 he carried out a bizarre and impressive effort towards patronage at local level, by transforming his government in an "intinerant administration" installed each time in a different region of Sao Paulo. Promises were made, support was searched and compromises were sometimes reached through a large use of "convenios" and the distribution of public jobs.[44]

The Maluf government which replaced the "infamous" and corrupt CECAP with a new public agency did not only do so to get rid of one of the most criticized public enterprises in the state of Sao Paulo. The new public enterprise had broader objectives than the previous one: to create new industrial centers in the interior of the state and reorganize existing ones. The program of popular housing would remain the same. These new tasks would be financed by reducing the number of employees from 634 to 280 and retaining the same budget of U.S. $7.6 million allocated to CODESPAULO by the state treasury. The principal problem which preoccupied the Maluf government was that 234 municipalities did not contribute to the state industrial sales tax (as they had no industry). In the opinion of Maluf's administration it was injust that in those cities that do not generate industrial sale taxes (ICM), the state should invest resources to create urban infrastructure, that is, construct popular housing and provide public services for the population.[45]

> The cities which do not generate economic products put the most pressure on the state government for subsidies and extra resources. Cities where an industrial nucleus exists are more independent. CODESPAULO should correct this disequilibrium.[46]

In the 234 municipalities that did not generate industrial sale taxes, at least one industry would be established. Later on a program of industrial relocation in medium sized cities in the Interior would be implemented. These and other urban projects were financed with the assistance of the BNH and the BNDE (National Development Bank). The government's primary objective was to modify the industrial profile of Sao Paulo as nobody contests the necessity to decentralize the industry in Sao Paulo.[47] According to Oswaldo Palmo (the State Secretary for Industry), CODESPAULO was established with the objective of being compatible with the necessities of industrial decentralization, especially in the Metropolitan Region of S.P. realizing that what exists today are satellite towns, without industries.[48]

In the state of Sao Paulo nearly 200 municipalities have no "industrial sales tax" (ICM Industrial) and CODESPAULO would encourage the development of industry thus increasing its 'Own Revenue' and diminishing its dependence on the federal transfers. Sao Paulo's revenue is heavily dependent on, 'Own Revenues'; 'Borrowing' and 'federal transferences', in that order. "Own Revenues"—mainly the sales tax (ICM)—are still the most important budegetary item, but have been decreasing, whereas "Federal Transfers" increased slowly from 1970 (3.75 percent) to 1978 (7.4 percent).[49] The sales tax benefits especially the more industrialized regions in Brazil and Sao Paulo has indeed one of the highest relations between the ICM and the "Own Revenues" in the country: an average of 79 percent between 1970 and 1979, against the 75 percent in Espirito Santo, 73 percent in Rio de Janeiro, and 63 percent in Bahia.[50]

During the Maluf government in the late 1970s the federal transfers to S.P. state were reduced to a record low: in 1978, it received U.S. $6.3 billions from its tax revenues from Sao Paulo and put back into the state only U.S. $430 millions.[51] Maluf, elected as governor of Sao Paulo state in 1979, did not have the support of either President Geisel, Governor Paulo Egydio or General Figueiredo and depended heavily on backing from right-wing businessmen and military hard-liners. The nomination of Maluf divided the PDS party and also aggravated Sao Paulo's conflict with the center.

During this period, the state government rationalized the public sector by eliminating the duplicity of functions and dismantling three loss making state enterprises: BRASVACIN; SETASSA; and CECAP. The byproduct of Maluf's 'rationalization' policies was that CODESPAULO (formerly CECAP) was left for nearly two years without financial aid from the BNH. Sao Paulo's governor did not foresee that with the dismantling of CECAP, the state would stop receiving from the federal government the necessary resources for the construction of housing projects. The loss of federal funds was also because of Maluf's lack of support at the Presidential level as he was nominated governor against the wishes of General Figueiredo. The President of the Republic disliked the methods employed by the ex-Prefect of Sao Paulo to win support from members of the ARENA party (see chapter 4). CECAP was the only financial agent of the BNH in the state government's field of action and with its extinction, the pact with the BNH was cancelled.

TABLE 3.3   Construction Position of CODESPAULO

Units Built (1967-80):	20,275
Units in Construction:	5,441
Units Planned for 1981:	38,601
Municipalities Attended - 1967/80:	119
Value of the 1981 Program (UPC):	6,896,914
Median Value of Unit Built in 1980 (UPC):	354

Source: CODESPAULO records

During the period of 1979–82, without federal resources Sao Paulo's state housing company was limited to finishing the construction of previous projects and even then restrictions imposed on various sectors of the state government caused difficulties in the transferring of funds.

CODESPAULO and CECAP suffered from similar problems. In the state circuit they had to compete with the "Caixa Economica Estadual's housing program"—Nosso Teto—that was given priority by the Maluf administration. In addition it had to look for new alternatives in order to differentiate from programs already realized by COHAB (Capital) and INOCOOP (State). One of Camargo's tasks was to initiate new and unique characteristics for CODESPAULO. With the election of a new state governor—Jose Maria Marin—the president and the financial director of CODESPAULO were dismissed by the Secretary for Industry, Oswaldo Palmo, because of their negligence. In 1982, following the direct elections for state governors, Franco Montoro—the new Paulista governor who is a member of the opposition party PMDB—decided that two of CODESPAULO's ex-directors would be prosecuted. Ismael Armond and Fernando Ribeiro de Valles were accused of maladministration that resulted in the dissolution of the state company. After having worked with Paulo Egydio, Armond collaborated with the ex-governor Paulo Maluf, as director of FEPASA. According to CODESPAULO's lawyer, the two ex-directors commercialized or gave authority to sell, during the fiscal year of 1977, a group of 25 housing projects at prices inferior to their cost, generating a loss of Cr$38,653,617.[52]

Most of the projects carried out until 1981 were in the interior of Sao Paulo state. Only a very small percentage of the units were constructed in the capital of the latter. Of the 32,000 units constructed between the period 1967 and 1983, nearly half were financed by the BNH. The remaining 53 percent were financed by the State of Sao

Paulo's Building Society—CEESP (Caixa Economica do Estado de Sao Paulo). The units under construction in 1983 were totally financed by the BNH. In recent years the only large project constructed by CO-DESPAULO in GSP was in Guaralhos. Almost 5000 units of an area of 60 square meters were sold to a population with an average income of 5 minimum salaries. By 1982 the last of these housing units had been acquired by applicants. With the election of the opposition government in the state of Sao Paulo the role of CODESPAULO in the "Paulista" housing market has diminished not only because of the BNH's diversion of funds to "pro-government" states (especially in the North East of Brazil) but also because of the Montoro government's lack of confidence in the administrative capabilities of CODESPAULO, thus diverting state housing resources to the COHABs. One of the ways of competing with the various public housing agencies for financial resources is to look for new alternatives in order to differentiate oneself from COHAB/SP and INOCOOP. Although CODESPAULO has serious financial and political problems (lack of support by the BNH or the state government) it has one of the largest public reserves of land in the state capital. In the area of Guaralhos is held a reserve of 935,000 square metres: in Ferraz de Vas Conselos—251,000 square metres; and in Santo Andre—1,500,000 square metres. This enormous reserve of land which is mostly near industrial estates could in the future enable CODESPAULO to re-enter on a large scale the "Paulista" public housing market.

Administrating Social Resources to Trade Unions

Political Methods of Controlling the Labor Movement

One of the most commonly mentioned strains on military regimes is the trade unions. The regulations and political ambitions of the unions are often in conflict with those of the military government. The Brazilian labor movement in general provides an excellent example of the co-optation policy of the patrimonial state. Rather than allow the growth of an independent and perhaps destabilizing labor movement, each regime since 1930 has used its power to tie labor to the government, effectively precluding the creation of an autonomous, politically active interest group to represent workers' concerns.[53]

After the 1930 coup, Vargas identified labor as a potential source of support for his regime. He not only interfered in trade union organizational efforts but also tied labor legally to the federal government. Trade unions were recognized legally and new ones created. During this period a number of strikes impaired the early years of the govern-

ment. In 1934, the Constitution outlawed strikes and the police supervised the labor movement. By 1937 any hint of an independent labor
movement had disappeared. As of 1937, with the enunciation of a new
trade union policy under the "Estado Novo", parallel organizations for
employers and employees were formed. This structure was never fully
applied to employers but is still imposed on workers today. The present
structure of trade union organization was set prior to the military
takeover by a labor code patterned on Mussolini's Carta del Lavoro
and elaborated in 1943. After 1964, the military regime modified certain
aspects and applied the controls with full severity.

Labor legislation ensured absolute control of the national state over
the activities of rural and urban labor unions. Trade unions are corporatively organized in such a way as to eliminate the possibility of
local horizontal union federations across sectors. Separate national confederations are established for industry, commerce, transport, and so
on. Only at the confederation level may the various occupational group-
ings establish formal connections. The structure of the syndicates served
the interests of the state with the maintenance of control over employees,
independent of the ideology of those in power. During periods of more
liberal and democratic governments depending on the popular vote, the
most severe restrictions and penalties were not applied, but those
measures were never eliminated. The military regime hardly altered
the legislation, changing only a few laws which helped to meet the
objectives of a "National Security State". The trade unions are organized
in a pyramid structure, to avoid the horizontal organization of the
different occupational categories. According to the Labor Laws, it is
prohibited to establish bodies that coordinate syndicates at a local level.
Thus, a local syndicate of steel workers cannot formally and legally
coordinate activities with bankers, employees of public transport services or any other syndicate. It can merely reunite with other syndicates
of the same category as its federation (see Figure 3.2). Only at the top,
through the confederation can all the categories of the same economic
sector formally coordinate. The vertical organizational structure objective assures centralization at the level of federations and confederations.

Apart from structural controls, the Ministry of Labor has other
means to control the activities of the trade unions. The state has the
right to intervene directly by replacing elected directors; the government
has the final say in the legal recognition of syndicates, can create other
unions and dissolve syndicates, thus forming obstacles to the latters'
liberal activities. Another method of control is through the unions
whose income is drawn from a compulsory salary deduction of all
Brazilian employees (including non-union members) and is directly
transferred to the government. Governmental institutions and the Bank

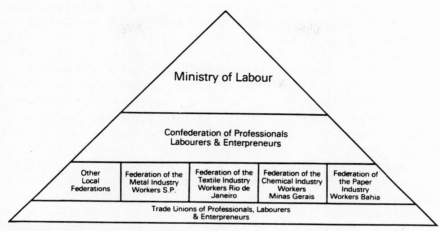

FIGURE 3.2 Structure of the Trade Unions

of Brazil decide on how to allocate the funds. The syndicates are allowed to spend funds on education and medical programs but not on political participation, strikes or financial support of political parties. In reality the trade unions were transformed into "social welfare" organizations, in many instances liberating the central government from social obligations.[54]

With the deprivation of the powerful manipulative relationship between the unions and the Goulart government it was necessary to introduce a new instrument of patronage.

A major element of the new housing project—the cooperative housing project—was to be channelled through unions which were prepared to collaborate with and were acceptable to the new government. In effect the program represented one way of selectively benefiting the membership of the unions and at the same time of offering an instrument of patronage to the new and often imposed union leadership.[55]

One of the major categories of recipients of the public housing programs is the trade unionists. Although conspirators took office without fully developed economic plans, the unions received quick attention from the new military government. Within the first month after the coup, forty labor leaders were replaced, including the heads of the National Confederation of Industrial Workers, the General Labor Command, the National Confederation of Workers in Agriculture and the National Confederation of Workers in Establishments of Credit. By the end of May the government admitted intervening in the 300 unions, including almost all important national unions. Overt opposition to these interventions was extremely rare. The military regime after 1964 implemented the right to intervene in trade unions with severity. Considering that by 1969 the government had intervened and removed from office the directors of a total of 999 unions, this amounted to a forced change of leadership in 50 percent of the unions existent at that time.

One of the various programs of the BNH was the provision of cooperative housing, initiated in May 1966. Consequently a "Plan for the Finance of Labourers' Cooperatives" was formed. The legislation also compelled the Bank to provide technical assistance to the cooperatives which were adjutant to the "Institutes for the Orientation of Housing Cooperatives" (INOCOOPS). The initial directorship of INOCOOP were members of the anti-communist Association of Christian Employers (DCI), an entity which congregated employers from all over Brazil. This was a step that offered some counterweight to "communist influence" in the trade unions.

> Perhaps more important, politically, than the provision of cooperative housing was the publicity and recruitment associated with the program. BNH officials and representatives of the new state-based but private cooperative institutes toured trade unions, announced the scheme, opened inscriptions and grouped applicants into cooperatives. The unions themselves were involved less as organizers and more as channels for recruitment. Indeed the intention was clearly not to let the cooperatives fall into the control of the unions or even, it might be said, of the cooperatives themselves.[56]

Financial Resources and the Administrative Process

The INOCOOPs' objective is to orientate the cooperatives in all the necessary operations for the construction of housing projects. This assistance is financed by charging a rate of 4 percent to 6 percent on the value of the cooperatives' project. These cooperatives are civil societies without profit aims, autonomous and independent, subject to the National Law of Cooperatives.[57] If at the end of a large project, for example, a profit was realized larger than expected by the INOCOOP, 20 percent of this surplus is distributed between the administration's employees while the remaining 80 percent is returned to the BNH's cooperative fund. The structure of the housing finance system for trade unions works in the following way:

1. INOCOOP locates a plot of land;
2. A project is developed and planned;

3. A construction firm from the private market is selected;
4. The cost of a housing unit is calculated;
5. According to the cost of a unit, INOCOOP, makes public the project as a means of finding clients—that is families with a sufficient monthly income to pay the mortgage;
6. A waiting list of potential candidates is formed;
7. A cooperative is created from candidates who meet the specific conditions of the new project;
8. The BNH examines the "package" and approves the project if it meets its parameters;
9. If the latter approves, then a loan financed by the BNH will be allocated to the cooperative;
10. BNH transfers the monetary funds to the financial agent (e.g., Caixa Economica Federal; Banespa) who in many cases supplements money to the loan;
11. The loan is transferred to the cooperative who then purchases the land and signs a contract with the construction firm and with INOCOOP;
12. When housing units are ready the distribution process to individuals is initiated;
13. The cooperative is dismantled.

Much of this complex procedure arose from BNH's requisite, as the source of funds, to ensure at all stages the financial and political viability and the marketability of the operation. INOCOOP itself has no direct access to the financial resources and is dependent on them. The first stage of finding a plot of land is not always in an area which INOCOOP thinks will meet the demands of the cooperative members. In quite a few instances, BNH donates land directly to INOCOOP (and also to COHAB) or it is purchased from other state agencies. Sometimes a construction firm will itself select a plot, mount a whole project and bring it forward to INOCOOP for examination. As of 1975, INOCOOP/ SP, purchased complete housing projects. This was the phase of purchasing large "ready made estates" which benefited the huge construction firms who supply INOCOOP with their surplus of housing units.[58] This surplus from the private housing market was sold to INOCOOP/ SP even though these projects were not only designated for the "working class" market or even for the middle income strata. This can explain the public campaigns carried out by INOCOOP/SP, in a similar procedure to the private real estate and construction firms and also the later decisions by the BNH authorizing "special conditions" for many of these projects. These special conditions consist basically of extension of the time of payment with the consequent reduction in the monthly income from the candidate thus guaranteeing the commercialization of the property. Since its foundation and until 1975, the BNH invested Cr$67 billion (more than US $10 billion) in its programs. According to the bank's own information, the "social area"—its principal aim— received 34.5 percent of this total.[59]

The latter investment which the bank claims to have been channeled to low income housing projects was artificially exaggerated when compared with what was actually invested to benefit low income families.[60] "Social interest" is only a figure of speech used by the bank to couple the popular housing schemes with the lower middle income projects. Up to 1975, a total of Cr$16 billion, or two thirds of the BNH's social interest budget, was allocated to the finance of housing programs for middle sector cooperatives, for private institutes of social welfare and for military credit foundations.

Only 9 percent of the BNH's budget was allocated to families with an income range of one to five minimum salaries. Only from 1975 onwards, due to a saturation of the demand for high income property, were slightly larger funds invested in low income housing. INOCOOP/ SP constructed in Greater Sao Paulo up to 1982 a total of 30,000 houses and apartments. The latter figure can be compared to the 90,000 units built by COHAB (up to 1979) and the 34,000 units constructed by CODESPAULO (up to 1980). The number of units constructed for cooperatives is relatively high if we take into consideration that INO-COOP builds more expensive units at an average cost of 1750 UPC (1983 prices) in GSP and 1350 UPC in the interior of the state (COHAB supplies housing at an average price of 800 UPC). While INOCOOP provides housing for a population with an average income of 6.6 minimum salaries (in GSP) and CODESPAULO at an average of 5.5 minimum salaries, COHAB constructs for a population with an income range of 1.5 to 6 minimum salaries. Most of INOCOOP's construction was carried out during the late 1970s, a period when independent trade union opposition emerged. In the middle of 1978, another decisive factor exploded in the Brazilian political scene. The first large worker strikes in ten years had begun mainly in Santo Andre, Sao Caetano and Diadema, the dense industrial belt around Sao Paulo known as the ABC, the heart of Brazil's industry. The strikes spread like an epidemic. In the space of two months, half a million workers at some 400 factories in 18 towns in Sao Paulo state tested their strength in strike action, Law No.4330, introduced by the military regime in 1964 to outlaw strikes, had in practice been overturned.[61]

A substantial proportion of INOCOOP's production was constructed in the South East region of Brazil: 60 percent out of a total production of 461,000 units (up to November 1983); in the Northern region of

Brazil—3 percent; in the South region—15 percent; in the North East—18 percent; and the Western region—7 percent. Sao Paulo and Rio de Janeiro were allocated more than 40 percent of the total INOCOOP production (shared equally between them). The main reason for this distributional pattern is the importance of the latter states not only as large industrial and public sector employers but also as a political force. Not only were there industrial strikes during the late 1970s but also public sector employees, hit by inflation, involved themselves in strikes. Sao Paulo municipal workers, teachers and doctors established employee associations as most public sector workers are not normally members of trade unions. Although the federal government wields great power over the state governments it could damage its public prestige if it engaged in open dispute with an important state government such as Sao Paulo. By investing in schemes such as cooperative housing, the government makes sure that despite the opposition parties' majority in the Congressional elections they will have little influence over the way the country is governed (see Table 3.4).

The federal Ministers of Interior, Labor and Treasury signed an agreement, in January 1980, for the execution of a "National Housing Program for Unionized Labour" (PROSINDI). The initial intentions were to guarantee housing for workers with a family income of up to six minimum salaries by means of land donated by the federal union, states and municipalities. The Minister of Labor—Murillo Macedo—declared that the main objective of the program (PROSINDI) was to strengthen the trade unions. He refuted the accusation that the program would be one more way of limiting the unions' autonomy, controlling the unions even more by the Labor Ministry. The president of the National Confederation of Workers in Credit Firms (CONTEC)—Wilson Gomes de Moura—also did not believe that PROSINDI would increase the ties of the Ministry of Labor to the unions. Rather, in his opinion, the trade unions were already controlled by the Ministry. This program would not diminish or increase this tie as long as the unions were not obliged to adhere. PROSINDI was developed through housing cooperatives, organized either on a local, regional or inter-statal basis. BNH would underwrite the necessary resources for PROSINDI by means of the Housing Finance System. One hundred thousand units at a cost of Cr$24 billion would be constructed during the 1980/85 period. According to the Minister Mario Andreazza, PROSINDI contemplated special financial conditions, in a way that permitted mortgage payments at a lower cost than renting housing, to a maximum of 20 percent of the monthly family income. Of the total INOCOOP/SP production in 1982, 47 percent were cooperative housing projects and 25 percent were PROSINDI programs.

TABLE 3.4 Number of Housing Units Constructed by INOCOOP - 1967/82.

YEAR	INTERIOR OF STATE	GSP	TOTAL
1967	560	432	992
1968	3313	2144	5457
1969	6141	306	6447
1970	2455	546	3001
1971	1691	1186	2377
1972	2167	1922	4089
1973	451	698	1149
1974	685	560	1245
1975	1500	464	1964
1976	1161	952	2113
1977	2068	2158	4226
1978	2522	1068	3950
1979	5803	5668	11461
1980	3296	5784	9080
1981	8073	1528	9601
1982	4658	3941	8599
Total	46544	29357	75901

The Allocation of Public Contracts

The issue of who gains benefits from public sector investments in construction is linked with the process of contracting for public works. Public housing agencies such as COHAB, INOCOOP and CODES-PAULO are in a strong and even dominant position to influence the development of the Brazilian construction industry. With the creation of the BNH in 1964, the potential for influence was apparently great as policies which were designed to affect the activities of the construction industry and its employment impact were formally stated. Besides attempts by the BNH to stimulate construction, these policies ranged in Brazil from the use of public investment to provide regional development and the contracting of regionally based firms, to the extension of credit to firms producing construction materials. Among the processes which comprise contracting practice in the three housing agencies are the formal rules of selection, but much more powerful are the informal procedures of selection which operate through administrative complexity, the terms of contract and the more or less private practices of particular agencies.

The Formal Rules

There are quite a lot of differences between COHAB, INOCOOP and CODESPAULO in the formally established procedures for contracting. COHAB has a more rigid and detailed practice in the elaboration of laws and regulations than INOCOOP as the former is a public agency subject to the scrutiny of the BNH, the press and the public. Before any firm could be contracted the three agencies required that the former should be formally registered. Only COHAB set out rules for the publication of information on contracts for tender, for tendering procedures and for the means of selecting between candidate firms. INOCOOP did not publicize information on contracts for tender and it chose the firm according to price factors. As opposed to COHAB, construction firms bring forward to the INOCOOP administrators a proposed project that includes even the plot of land. The latter then decides if this project is appropriate for its candidates. In a situation like this no public tenders are published. Only when land is sold or donated by state or federal institutions does INOCOOP tender for the construction. COHAB/SP as well as CODESPAULO select construction firms only by means of a public tender.

The Informal Rules

Various elements in the conditions on which contracts are offered tend to operate in favour of larger, better-established firms. By restricting the number of firms entering the constructing process, the reputation and experience of the construction corporations are advanced. Investment in public works contributes to the concentration of the development of the construction industry. The dominance of a small number of large firms in the Brazilian construction industry resulted from the restricted contracting practice which protects a reserved number of selected and well-known companies which are or become large and sophisticated in their operations. During the early and mid-1970s, a period of high demand, large construction firms concentrated on investing their capital in expensive housing for the middle and upper income sectors. As during that period they could hold out for concessions on profits before committing capital, few low income houses were financed by the state housing agencies. It was only in the late 1970s and early 1980s, a period of saturation in the high and middle income sectors' demand for housing, that the balance of market power switched back to public housing agencies. Most of the large Paulista public housing projects were constructed during that era (see Chapter 4).

As the cost levels of public works are mostly regulated by the housing agencies, big construction firms have demanded large package deal contracts. Large corporations have also exerted pressure not only to increase the unit size of investment but to construct industrialized flats. Thus although the Itaquera housing units were initially constructed using traditional methods (stage I of Itaquera) at a later stage of this project (stage II/III of Itaquera) technological sophistication was stressed as a way to insulate competition from smaller firms. The large construction corporations exerted pressure on COHAB and INOCOOP to accept their view that systems-building would rapidly become the dominant mode within the house-building sector, particularly for the public sector. CODESPAULO did not employ these methods as their housing is cheaper than that of the above agencies. In contrast to the other two, they built mainly outside GSP where the land is cheaper and thus it is more profitable to employ mainly traditional construction methods. Systems-building, it was said, aimed to reduce the demand for on-site craft skills by increasing the proportion of factory-produced components and by increasing the scale of site mechanization.

Six large firms which constructed most of the public housing in GSP during the 1970s and 1980s argued that although the saving of site labor would be partially off-set by an increase in factory labor, substantial overall economies were possible. The move by these firms (Jau, Better, Schahin Cury, Oxford, Sergus, Arauju) towards factory production, greater fixed capital requirements on site and the "de-skilling" of the labor force, helped them to outcompete the small and medium-sized builders. Although these firms succeeded in convincing the public housing agencies that substantial savings would be possible, it seems clear that it is by no means easy to develop systems of factory-built construction which are more economic of resources than traditional forms of construction. By comparing the prices of housing units built in the first stages of Itaquera (built in a traditional method) to those of Itaquera II/III we can conclude that system-building is at best only marginally cheaper than traditional forms. As some of the later unit costs increased (due to the high unit costs of prefabricated units if the level of demand does not permit high capacity utilisation within the factory) a larger than expected proportion of the units were sold to middle income sectors of the population (see Chapter 4).

Other larger firms responded to this saturation in the private sector of the housing market by diverting capital into lucrative foreign markets (mainly the Middle East and Africa). Firms like Construtora Mendes Junior and PROMON played major civil engineering and consulting roles in most of the major projects in Brazil: the Itaipu and Parana basin project; the controversial Brazilian nuclear power program; the gigantic iron ore mining/port complex at Carajas; the development of the Metro systems for both Sao Paulo and Rio de Janeiro; and a host of other smaller construction projects throughout the country. With experience of major civil projects, built up over the past 25 years, Brazil's construction industry is beginning to find a significant role to play in Third World projects as most of the major public works in Brazil have already been built and the public sector does not award new ones due to its large deficit. As large firms divert an ever increasing proportion of their capital into lucrative overseas markets, public housing work partially reverted to smaller companies.

A Concluding Note

Brazil, like many other developing countries has undergone a large expansion of governmental activity accompanied by a proliferation of official agencies and functions. As in many third world countries the public sector is the largest employer. By 1979 the state government (S.P.) comprised some 65 decentralized agencies. Between them, 32 were public enterprises, 22 were "autarquias" and 11 were foundations.[62] These agencies employed more than 100,000 functionaries in the mid-1970s, making them the second largest employers in Brazil—the federal government employed 353,405 civil servants during this period. They spent nearly 40 percent of the state government budget in 1976; most of the state governmental investment was channelled through the latter; they were active in a great variety of sectors: transportation; energy; infrastructure services; finance; education; health; agriculture, technology and science; urban and regional planning; welfare; tourism and housing.

Governments have both economic and political interests for investing so heavily in the public sector. In furthering national economic and political policies, as well as in furthering the interests of politically dominant social groups, public enterprises are frequently used as instruments for carrying out these aims. CECAP throughout its two decades of existence, invested in public housing programs while furthering the political policies of the state governments. During elections, state agencies such as the latter participated actively, if not always directly, in the political campaigns. The construction and marketability of housing units by CECAP seemed to be a secondary issue, as during the period 1965/79 only 18,000 were constructed. This was one of the reasons that supporters and opponents of the political leadership of Sao Paulo state were concerned with CECAP's activities and were anxious to influence it and hold it to account. This kind of accountability, however, may have little to do with the successful operation of public enterprises. Supporters may be seeking advantages from them (such as a "patronage" role) rather than state or national interest.

Unfortunately, there are widespread examples of inefficiency, ineffectiveness, and political corruption in Brazilian public enterprises. Too many government corporations were set up without taking responsible action to assure the support of management capabilities and public accountability. The proliferation of public enterprises, with some governmental authority over the allocation and use of economic resources (e.g., public housing) provides political parties with the means of inducing political conformity, as contracts for example may go only as a reward to the party faithful.

> The problem of corruption in the public enterprise sector can be partially reduced by abolishing the sector and assigning its operations to the private enterprise. Some countries, however, have ideological objections to this course, or recognize that there are several forms of public enterprise which do not lend themselves to private ownership or management or which are not attractive to private investment.[63]

Brazil, with a historical tradition of state involvement in the economy (see Chapter 2) did not yet advocate such a reform in the public enterprise sector.

A consequence of the 1982 state government elections was the changes in the administration and directorship of the state and municipal enterprises which would adhere to the PMDB's economic and social policies. The newly appointed mayor of GSP—Mario Covas—started his public career in 1961 as Secretary of Labor in Santos. After being elected in 1962 as a federal deputy by the labor party (Partido Social Trabalhista) he helped found the Brazilian Democratic Movement (MDB) in 1965. In the early 1980s he was responsible for the organisation of PMDB's party directories in 501 of the 572 municipalities of the S.P. state. Housing is one of the priorities of the mayor's new government, that intends to initiate the occupation of empty urban land; acquire land in areas that already have infrastructure in order to offer popular housing in regions nearer to the city center; stimulate private initiative to construct for low income residents; increase the supply of low cost plots.[64]

Mario Covas, whose administration took office in 1983, not only had to strive with federal government cuts in state transfers and with inflationary problems but also with the vast debits left behind by the previous Maluf government. Since 1979, the municipality's own resources began to diminish and borrowing money became more difficult. In 1983, with the prefecture having severe financial difficulties, investment in public works was reduced from 20 percent of the budget to a mere 8 percent. Although with a budget of Cr$1.118 trillion, Sao Paulo still has the fifth largest budget in the country, this amount is insufficient to supply public services to the city's 9.5 million inhabitants. With 25 percent of the municipality's budget paying back previous debts and an increase in the payroll of the functionaries it was necessary to cut back in investments in public housing and infrastructural works.

The budget was calculated on a basis of an inflation of 130 percent while five months later it reached 211 percent—complained the municipal secretary of finance. If we look from above, the guilty one is the federal government: we are confronting various obstacles and the majority are of a political nature. For example, the extreme concentration of the tax reform system, that is a structural phenomenon, permits the federal government to control larger and larger resources. State and municipalities are the prejudiced ones. The repercussions are political, as opposition governments were elected; they suffer the impact of the economic enclosure.[65]

If Brasilia is interested in demoralizing the governor or the prefect, they tighten the screws of transferring federal resources internally, or do not endorse foreign loans. Without the endorsement no foreign bank will loan to Sao Paulo's government. Mario Covas complained bitterly against the "enclosure" (by the federal government) claiming that S.P. did not receive more than 1 percent of the BNH resources for the municipality while the BNH in Sao Paulo attracts nearly 25 percent of the FGTS. Thus it would be fair to invest at least 8 percent in Sao Paulo. Although Mario Covas presented to the BNH an "emergency housing plan" requesting finance for 45,000 regular units and 10,000 "self help" units (PROMORAR), he did not receive any official reply. Covas denounced the BNH's intention of transforming Sao Paulo into a city of "fourth category" (in BNH financial terms) and declared that while the municipality repaid to the BNH Cr$6 billion, a sum of Cr$8.6 billion which the bank owes the city was refuted by alleging the organ's non-compliance with its terms. This attitude of the federal government toward Sao Paulo is a discrimination. The prefect also criticized BNH policy of financing the construction of luxury housing, while refusing to finance popular housing in a city where 54 percent live in sub-normal dwellings. The financing of housing for the middle sectors in Sao Paulo is part of a wider governmental policy of investing in social programs as a means of averting threats to its stability or existence. Although the military regime was interested in developing the necessary sense of legitimacy it did not opt to actually share its power. Rather a strategy of co-opting the trade unions and mobilizing patron-client alliances with the middle sectors was chosen.

The distributional process of housing in COHAB, CODESPAULO and INOCOOP is an example of a situation where the state apparatus monopolizes economic and social power in the society and retains full discretion over policy initiatives. Commonly in such organisations, the policies respond generally to the institutional interests of the politicians who dominate the municipal, state and federal governments. The part on CODESPAULO provides an example how a clientelistic type of regime (e.g., during Maluf's administration) may embark on housing programs to win votes and support from other politicians. The analysis of public housing agencies in GSP indicates that housing policy became a tool to be used in clientelist fashion to allocate awards in the political system. The provision of housing to public employees and to privileged groups in the "modern" sectors of Brazil is typical of countries with a longstanding tradition of corporate structures. Although these groups and classes do not generate policy alternatives nor determine their outcome, they generate demands and form coalitions. Given the limits on the government's economic capability, resources allocated to one group or sector cannot be invested in another, even though the regime may announce uniformly high priority for most of its housing programs. Although the political leadership makes periodic decisions about the priority of each sector of the population, system-threatening distur-bances in some sectors (e.g., industrial strikes in the ABC region of S.P. during the late 1970s) may draw a sudden influx of resources to attend to the crisis, draining money from other programs.

The Political Feasibility of Public Housing Policies

A major question running through this study concerns the pressures in Brazil which led military governments to redistribute housing ser-vices and costs in such a way as to confer greater benefits on middle and upper income sectors than on lower and more needy income sectors. By investigating the development of housing in Sao Paulo, our study provides evidence indicating that in many crucial respects the state has politically administered its welfare programs. Public housing programs were used to maintain income levels among groups of workers (mainly middle sectors) despite the vicissitudes of the market. Although the military-dominated authoritarian regime which emerged in 1964 formulated programs to expand coverage and rescheduling benefits so as to increase general social equity, these have not been implemented. Rather, such programs have increased the power of administrative technocratic elites. In addition, these programs along with others, were political acts that increased the bargaining power of key groups such as organized white-collar workers in the urban sector (mainly INO-COOP programs for trade unionists). The adoption of a public housing program in Brazil theoretically opened a new and important arena for mass participation. However, the history of the early housing agencies (see Chapter 2) reveals a particularistic, piecemeal approach. For the most part, these early programs (e.g., The Foundation for Popular Housing) granted protection to designated social sectors usually identified and defined in terms of economic function and/or occupational criteria. With the incremental growth of new BNH funds (e.g., the FGTS) the general pattern was to move towards newly recognized groups: from military and civil public employees (e.g., 1960s subsidized high-rise housing for the military constructed in the place of evacuated favelas in Rio de Janeiro), to those employed in critical urban services and in industrial activities (see chapter 4).

Public housing programs in Brazil (and in many other developing countries) were not designed to embrace the masses as a whole. Housing policies, such as those of the INOCOOP, developed by accretion as the government granted specific programs to specific working groups who were perceived to have the actual or potential power to threaten the system. Thus, public sector employees in Sao Paulo received privileges in the allocation process of state housing (see Chapter 4). The inequities arising from existing housing programs have not only come about through the interaction of organized groups with the state. There also has been an administrative and political logic in the functioning of public housing agencies in Brazil. Once in place, the pattern of program growth reflected administrative logic: the state and municipal agencies sought out clienteles, especially those employed by public organizations and trade unions, who were readily identifiable and financially strong. This latter factor reduced the risk of default in mortgage payments. The administrative logic behind Paulista housing policies made it easier to administer organized workers in the modern market sector than urban marginals. Low-income groups were excluded from most of the public housing program because they lacked political clout and were not administratively "attractive". As in other countries, Brazilian "working-class groups generally have a better access if a left-wing government is in office, middle-sector and business groups (e.g., large construction corporations) get better hearing from a right-wing government.[66] In sum, the structural objectives of the Paulista housing programs and the political context intially converged to create highly inequitable policies.

Notes

1. J. Love, *Sao Paulo in the Brazilian Federation* (Stanford: Califorinia University Press, 1980).
2. Peter Flynn, *Brazil—A Political Analysis* (London: E. Benn, 1978).
3. L. Coutinho, "Administracao Descentralizada em Sao Paulo", in *Revista de Administracao de Empresas* (Rio de Janeiro: June 1979).
4. See Outline Structure of the Housing Finance System.
5. E. Camargo, "O Desenvolvimento das Favelas na GSP", in *Problemas Brasileiros* (Brazil: May 1983).
6. *Ibid*, p. 89.
7. O Estado de Sao Paulo, *Banco Mundial Financia 20,000 Casas Populares em Sao Paulo* (20/9/1978).
8. Richard Batley, *Power Through Bureaucracy* (London: Gower, 1983), p. 155.
9. *Ibid.*
10. Werner Baer, *The Brazilian Economy* (USA: Praeger, 1983), p. 123.
11. Interview with Ubirajara (Architect at COHAB/SP).
12. During this period a substantial number of construction firms collapsed.
13. O Estado de Sao Paulo, *BNH: Mais de 50% Atrasa Prestacao* (18/8/1979).
14. O Estado de Sao Paulo, *Apos 15 Anos, Persistem Falhas do SFH*(9/9/1979).
15. Richard Batley, *op. cit.*, p. 144.
16. Based on 7/1/1982 figures: Cr$252 = US1$.
17. This part based on *Documentacao de Orientacao aos Dirigentes de COHABs* (Rio de Janeiro: BNH, 1983).
18. O Estado de Sao Paulo, *O Problema Habitacional*(18/8/1982).
19. Allan Gilbert, "Housing in Latin America", in Herbert and Johnston *Geography and the Urban Environment* (USA: Wiley, 1980), p. 2851.
20. O Estado de Sao Paulo, *Casas Populares, O Sonho Fragil e Caro* (17/4/1983).
21. *Ibid.*
22. *Ibid.*
23. R. Batley, *Power*, p. 129.
24. A special state housing agency was created only in 1982—Montoro's government.
25. Sao Paulo State Secretary of Planning and Economy, *Manifestacoes da Relacao Estado—Urbano no Estado de Sao Paulo* (February 1979).
26. Journal da Tarde, *Baldacci se Defende* (27/1/1977).
27. Sao Paulo State Secretary of Planning and Economy, *op. cit.*
28. *Ibid.*

29. See part on COHAB and Chapter 4.
30. Journal do Brasil, *Vice Prefeito Accusa CECAP* (25/1/1977).
31. Journal da Tarde, *Baldacci se Defende* (27/1/1977).
32. O Estado de Sao Paulo, *Egydio Quer Que ARENA de Apoio a CEI* (29/1/1977).
33. *Ibid.*
34. Journal da Tarde, *Outro Depoimento Contra Baldacci* (18/3/1977).
35. O Estado de Sao Paulo, *Klabin Deixa CECAP e Acusa Maluf* (11/7/1980).
36. *Ibid.*
37. *Ibid.*
38. *Ibid.*
39. *Ibid.*
40. O Estado de Sao Paulo, *Presidente de CECAP* (18/7/1980).
41. Interview with Dr. Z. Macedo: Planner at EMPLASA (December 1983).
42. O Estado de Sao Paulo, *Polos Industriais Nos Planos de CODESPAULO* (21/1/81).
43. *Ibid.*
44. A.C. de Medeiros, *Inter-Governmental Relations in Brazil* (London School of Economics: unpublished PhD, 1983).
45. Folha de Sao Paulo, *No Lugar do CECAP Uma Empresa Para o Interior* (28/1/1981).
46. *Ibid.*
47. *Ibid.*
48. O Estado de Sao Paulo, *Criada Empresa Para Substituir CECAP* (20/1/1981).
49. Medeiros, *Inter-Governmental*, Chapters 6 and 8.
50. *Ibid.*
51. *Ibid.*
52. O Estado de Sao Paulo, *Governo Procesa Antigos Diretores* (23/9/1983).
53. R. Roett, *Brazil: Politics in a Patrimonial Society* (USA: Praeger, 1978), p. 120.
54. M. Alves, *Estado e Oposicao no Brazil* (Petropolis: Vozes, 1984), p. 239.
55. R. Batley, *Power Through Bureaucracy* (London: Gower, 1983), Ch. 4.
56. R. Batley,*Ibid*, p. 78.
57. This part based on an interview with A.C. de Angelis, Director of Coordination and planning at INOCOOP/SP (31/1/1984).
58. S. Peruzzo, *Habitacao: Controle e Espoliacao* (Sao Paulo: Cortez Editoras, 1984), p. 53.
59. O Estado de Sao Paulo, *Aos 15 Anos Persistem as Falhas do SFH* (9/9/1979).
60. A. Portes, "Politica Habitacional, Pobreza e o Estado", in *Estudos CEBRAP* (No. 18, 1976).
61. B. Kucinski, *Brazil: State and Struggle* (London: Latin American Bureau, 1982), p. 67.
62. Medeiros, *op. cit.*

63. G. Shidlo, *An Analysis of Political Corruption in Developing Countries* (London School of Economics: Unpublished MSc. Thesis, 1982), p. 31.

64. Associacao Brasileira de COHABs, *Habitacao Popular* (Rio de Janeiro, June 1983), p. 135.

65. O Estado de Sao Paulo, *Pobre Cidade de Cr$1 Trillion* (22/1/84).

66. B. Heady, *Housing Policy in the Developed Economy* (Kent: Croom Helm, 1978), p. 34.

4

The Consumption of Social Resources by the Middle Sectors

Introduction

Itaquera is not typical of the public housing projects of Brazil; no single settlement could possibly be that, given the large number of units built. But this large settlement of some 30,000 families, situated in the east zone of Greater Sao Paulo, is probably representative of those smaller middle income housing projects built by the various COHABs lying within the city. The socio-economic structure of the population of Itaquera is probably not dissimilar to those of thousands of others living in the vast peripheral settlements. The district of Itaquera possesses 58 square kilometres and is 18 kilometres from the centre of Sao Paulo. In the 1950s, the latter was predominantly a rural area. Until the 1970s, nearly half of the population was employed in agriculture. The changes occurred from 1980 onwards when a mere 6 percent of the inhabitants was engaged in agricultural activities. At the same time the number of inhabitants increased significantly—from 33,000 in 1960 to 444,000 in 1981. Even in 1970 the population of Itaquera represented 3 percent of the inhabitants of Sao Paulo city, in 1981 this increased to 6 percent. The increase in population is linked to the process of expansion of urban space of the Metropolitan area of Sao Paulo and also of public sector intervention in the housing market. Already in 1968, the Metropolitan Plan for Integrated Development (PMDI) recommended the occupation of the eastern zone of the city. The latter was indicated as the most suitable for expansion not only because of the availability of large quantities of land but also due to the proposal of the construction of a East-West Metro line. Another crucial factor which determined the decision to construct was the transfer of plots of urban land, belonging to the National Social Security Institute (INAMPS), to the BNH who in turn transferred them to COHAB/SP.

Politics in Sao Paulo and the Evolution
of the Urban Middle Sector

Since the 1970s

the Brazilian regime has adopted a strategy of authoritarian clientelism while looking for opportunities to bring about genuine political transformations. Elections have regularly been held for Congress and local "municipios" and the political opening was extended considerably further in November 1982 when state governors were elected directly.[1]

The analysis of two post-1964 governors of Sao Paulo (not elected directly)—Paulo Egydio Martins (1975–1979) and Paulo Salim Maluf (1979–1982)—will enable the examination of certain aspects of clientelistic politics by focusing on the allocation of state and municipal housing.[2]

The first two post-1966 appointed governors (in Sao Paulo state)—Roberto de Abreu Sodre (1967–1970) and Laudo Natel (1971–74)—were already men whose basic loyalty was directed to the center and whose priorities once in office were largely those of the centre. Still, their use of patronage to co-opt local allies—mainly Natel's—was far reaching.[3]

During the era of the Natel government, investment in public housing was not an important priority. Construction was mostly for the middle sectors as BNH resources were nearly all allocated for the latter sectors of the population.

The analysis of legislative elections since 1966 shows a clear trend of systematic losses by the government party (ARENA). In the elections of 1974, as part of his electoral campaign, Laudo Natel distributed over 3000 jobs in the state government administration. His main opponents for the governorship of Brazil's most economically active state were Delfim Netto and Paulo Egydio Martins. Netto intended to win the elections and use it as a bridgehead to the presidential appointment in 1978. Martins' candidacy had the strong and influential support of President Geisel who opposed Delfim's economic policies. Paulo Egydio had in the past been minister of industry and trade in the government of President Humberto Castelo Branco. Although Martin's lacked political support in the state, this was not crucial as the governor was elected by the state legislature which was securely in ARENA hands. But it is hard even for the President of Brazil entirely to ignore the will of Sao Paulo magnates and political leaders, many of whom are disposed to back Delfim's candidacy. Even "O Estado de Sao Paulo", which was fiercely opposed to the Medici administration (though not to its economic policies), believed that Delfim should be allowed to take his chance. The bankers and industrialists of Sao Paulo, who controlled the local ARENA party, made it clear that they wanted Delfim. This desire by the Paulistas for their own candidate went well beyond their confidence in Delfim—he was seen as a candidate for the presidential succession in 1979. This picture was further complicated by the emergence of yet another candidate for the governorship, senator Carlos Alberto Carvalho Pinto, whom Geisel wished to reserve for the senate for yet another term.

Carvalho Pinto joined the conspiracy against Joao Goulart in 1964 only at the last minute. He, too, would be a strong "civilista" candidate. He had already a term as Sao Paulo's governor—before 1964. Since 1964 he was the ARENA senator for Sao Paulo, but did not wish to seek re-election. Although public opinion polls, carried out by private polling organizations, showed that the popular choices for the governorship would be Delfim Netto or Carvalho Pinto, with Egydio Martins so far behind that he did not figure in the results, Geisel chose the latter candidate. Geisel's pressure on the ARENA party to appoint Martin's to this influential post was part of his "distensao" strategy. The President planned that his close colleague Martins would eventually be his civilian successor. During the electoral campaign a number of measures were taken with a view to increase the government's popularity. In the case of a 10 percent wage increase, the advice of an ARENA candidate was proclaimed as the origin of the change. Throughout the week before polling day the government authorised the building of a new sector of the Sao Paulo underground system and also determined that all buyers of houses through the BNH should be given back 10 percent of the payments made during the past year.

Martins' state government reactivated the quiet public housing market. Urban and housing plans were commissioned to survey housing demand and project future plans. An estimate of a deficit of one million housing units up to the year 1980 was made by the state Secretary of Economy and Planning.[4]

Throughout Martin's governorship criticism pointed towards the central government. Paulista bourgeoisie saw central government intervention as excessive. Second, central control lost its authority over the security apparatus. The phenomenon of bourgeoisie discontent, which grew steadily thereafter, came about when it began to be realized that there was a reduction of the "economic cake" to be divided.[5]

In response to the bourgeoisie's discontent with the state apparatus, Martin's adminstration decided to amplify the inadequate state housing system. Municipal and state housing agencies were reformed so to have capacity to execute government strategy, reduce the housing deficit, improve the existing units, increase the supply of units and reduce production costs. It was during this administration that the Itaquera project began to be planned. Paulo Egydio Martins, gave priority in the popular housing sector to the large urban centers.

Paulo Maluf's Urban Political Machine

Maluf's career as a politician started in the 1950s when he befriended the Commander of the Second Army (which is stationed in Sao Paulo)— General Arthur da Costa e Silva. His nomination to the post of director of the "Caixa Economica Federal" in 1967 as well as to the Mayorship of Brazil's largest city was due to Costa e Silva's political connections. A survey carried out before the municipal elections of 1969 showed the following results: 90 percent in favour of the continuation of Faria Lima as Mayor; 7 percent in favour of Laudo Natel; 1 percent for Herbert Levy; and Paulo Maluf nil. The last result demonstrates the importance of Maluf's links with Costa e Silva. During his period as Mayor of Sao Paulo and later as State Secretary of Transport (1971– 1975) Maluf had begun to build up a huge clientelist network of patronage to win over the necessary support of the party delegates and thus to become governor by beating the centre's candidate, Laudo Natel.[6]

In 1978, Maluf declared himself candidate for the state governorship thus opposing President Geisel and Laudo Natel—General Figueiredo's candidate for the post. During his campaign Maluf travelled not only in the interior of the state but also to the Northeast region of Brazil to gain support from the 1256 members of the ARENA party.

In a survey carried out by the "Journal do Brasil" before the party elections, a third of the members of Congress were in favour of Maluf. One of the largest "supporters" of Maluf was his opponent, Laudo Natel, who did not carry out an electoral campaign as he had the illusion that the ARENA deputies and senators would vote according to "instructions from above". Both President Geisel and General Figueiredo were quite irritated with the methods employed by the ex-Prefect Paulo Salim Maluf to "buy votes" from members of the Arenista convention. After offering his supporters chauffered limousines and accommodation in luxury hotels, Maluf awaited the final counting of the votes which gave him a lead of 28 votes on his opponent Laudo Natel who suffered a loss of 617 votes against 589 in the party convention. The leaders of the central government tried unsuccessfully to engineer the elections by requesting the Superior Electoral Tribunal to enquire and judge the validity of Maluf's victory.

On the 15th of March 1979, Maluf was nominated governor against the wishes of the federal government who opposed his nomination due to his link with the business community who sought to overthrow Geisel. The election of a new state governor brought forward not only policy changes but also a change of administration in the state's housing agencies. During the Maluf administration state and municipal housing companies (as well as other "autarquias") were expanded extensively from being mere instruments of government control to instruments of pressure for government favours to specific sectors of the population. During the late 1970s and early 1980s, the Paulista state machinery was transformed into a party orientated patronage system. The government was installed each time in a different area of the state.

During 1979 he carried out a bizarre and impressive effort towards patronage local level. Promises were made, support was searched and compromises were sometimes reached through a large use of 'convenios' and the distribution of jobs as part of the governor's strategy to seek support for his administration.[7]

The state governor in his numerous publicity campaigns throughout the interior of the state and the North East promised to allocate to his supporters public resources (e.g., public housing). Such allocation can also be analysed in clientelist-patronage terminology.

The Politics of Public Housing Allocation

An overwhelming characteristic of Third World countries is that large proportions of their populations live at below subsistence level, or only slightly above and the need for the goods and services promised by various government programs is great. At the same time, an increasing number of governments have chosen authoritarian solutions to the problems of managing political participation and conflict. This suggests that the capacity of low-income groups to acquire benefits from their governments may be strictly limited in an environment that minimizes the influence of numbers on political decision-making through the elimination of open elections and rotating leadership. The politics of resource allocation in Sao Paulo indicate the absence of effective channels through which the city's low income inhabitants could effect policy formulation and implementation. Our research examines the distributive process of one public housing agency nominally oriented to low income groups.

The Distributive Rules of COHAB Sao Paulo

Although the Metropolitan Housing Company is an autonomous agency, ninety-five percent owned by the Municipality, it is subject to nationally applicable BNH rules. According to the latter, candidates who are able to prove a family income of between twice and five times the minimum salary, who have lived or worked at least two years in GSP, who have their personal documentation in order and who have a family or dependents, are formally eligible to inscribe for COHAB housing.[8]

Unable to meet the immense demand from candidates who are able to satisfy the formal criteria, other means of discriminating between them have been introduced. Due to the ceiling of five minimum salaries the possibility of turning to market criteria does not exist—in other words COHAB cannot make important moves up market (as INOCOOP has done) to reduce demand (and risk).[9]

The chronic shortfall in the supply of housing required COHAB employees to discriminate among clients, distributing or withholding resources according to their own criteria rather than to purely technical rules. They simply could not attend to all of the citizens who rightfully deserved public housing. After the candidates had met the first set of formal eligibility conditions, they therefore faced a second set of conditions that assessed eligibility for a particular housing scheme rather than for municipal housing as a whole. COHAB required that candidates have enough to repay the mortgage scheme and not the officially necessary income of two minimum salaries—in 1976 that would be about three minimum salaries.

In spite of reselecting candidates, establishing exclusive financial criteria and requiring documentation of regularity of employment and the existence debts, COHAB still could not meet the large demand. Rather the candidates selected were those whose documents have most recently been shown to be in order and for whom there exists a current statement of income. This favors the most recently registered candidates, people who have had "political" introductions through the directorate (and who are kept in a special list) and those candidates who exert the most insistent pressure on COHAB.[10] Candidates desiring "special" attention from COHAB, therefore sought the assistance of politicians and bureaucrats with contacts or influence in the public housing apparatus. In other words, as political criteria had come to govern appointments within the system especially during the Maluf government, so political criteria came to determine who would receive benefits (this, as we will see later, greatly increased the political leverage of well-placed politicians and bureaucrats).

COHAB does not usually publicize the availability of housing to low income people. The great majority of candidates hear about COHAB through friends or, in the case of introduced candidates, through elected representatives, COHAB and BNH staff and employees. From the point of view of COHAB with its low capacity to supply, there is no point in activating demand by advertising or by informing failed applicants of their rights.[11]

According to an interview with a senior COHAB official not only was his own luxury house financed by the state but also his brother-in-law was given priority in the long waiting list for state subsidised mortgages. From its creation and to 1976, COHAB/SP discriminated by some means the allocation of housing as a consequence of over-whelming demand and low supply. Up to 1976, the latter had sold only 6000 units although there was a waiting list of hundreds of thousands of candidates. This can be explained not only because of rapidly rising land and material costs, the low purchasing power of clients, BNH limits on the sale price, but also the inefficiency, maladministration and corruption in COHAB's management. Founded in 1967, the latter agency was known as one of the least efficient and most corrupt agencies of the Paulista public sector. They even constructed a housing project of 1264 units, which was uninhabited for three years after its completion, simply because they forgot to install water supplies.[12]

Since 1975, with J. Bourroul as COHAB's president, more than one hundred thousand new units have been distributed, housing a population of more than half a million inhabitants. With the construction of large projects, such as Itaquera and St. Etelvina, the process of selecting candidates has been modernized. The initial selection procedure has been computerized. PRODAM, the municipality's data processing company, loans its information and skills to the latter agency. Although it was anticipated that the number of candidates in the selection list and the waiting time drastically reduced, due to increased supply and computerization of information, the result was contrary to expectation. According to COHAB officials there were 300,000 candidates in 1983 in the waiting list.[13] This is largely due to a new policy of inscribing a number of candidates at least two to three times larger than the actual potential supply (previously it was only one third more candidates than available housing units).

While in previous years candidates waited two years, they now wait three years before being offered housing (which even then is not always suitable to their original demands). The conditions for access (to the Itaquera project) were a family income of three to five minimum salaries (171–285 US dollars per month) and in the case of larger units, that the family be composed of at least five persons. Evidently those conditions were never rigorously maintained: on the one hand political interferences and administrative on the other, generated a degree of favoritism in acquisition rights as well as some violations in regard to the upper limit of income admitted.[14]

According to an official document which was circulated to COHAB candidates in November 1983, contrary to what had happened in the past, when families with a higher than five minimum salaries could not be attended, now all families with sufficient income to pay the mortgage repayments would be attended. The larger your family income the greater the chance to choose the better options, although this would also depend on the chronological order of your inscription in the waiting list (fila) and the number of family members.[15] The waiting list is used by state officials and politicians who often find themselves in the role of camouflaging specific housing policies by referring to the sacrosanct of the rules of the game. The line creates an illusion that all candidates will eventually be allocated public housing, thus contributing to social and political tranquility. This situation enables the regime both to remove the threat of political protest by "favelados" and prevent effective articulate middle-sector demands. Although only a small percentage of COHAB's construction is for the low income market, shantytown and slumdwellers believe they will eventually be allocated public housing. As in many other non-democratic regimes, the process in Brazil of determining who will receive public housing is influenced by clientelistic criteria.

An Analysis of the Socio-Economic Structure
of the Itaquera Population

Public policy studies have paid little attention to the composition of the population of public housing as a variable in political analysis. This omission would be suprising were it not for the fact that the basic descriptive data are normally not available. An analysis of recent results from the Sao Paulo State Institute of Technological Research (IPT) survey of the largest housing complex in Brazil—Itaquera—provides fresh insights into this aspect of Brazilian public policy. Recent publications of advanced tabulations from the national and state (Sao Paulo) census permits some explanatory analysis of the country's patterns of public housing policies. In general, the analysis suggests that, while there has been some progress in the construction of low-income housing, a substantial proportion of resources have been allocated to the middle-income sector of society (especially in the South East region of Brazil).

As part of the government's policy to eradicate "favelas" from well-located and valuable land, a few hundred houses were specially constructed for "ex-favelados" in Itaquera. By integrating shantytown and slumdwellers in a middle sector housing project the regime believed that a potential threat of political disruption would be removed.

Geographical Distribution

Brazilians view the country as having five major regions quite distinct in physiography, history, population distribution and economic development. The origin of the Itaquera population is unevenly distributed. All the regions are under-represented, except for Sao Paulo (metropolitan region and interior of state) and the North East which are heavily overrepresented. Thirty percent of the inhabitants migrated from the poverty-stricken North East while fifty two percent originate from Sao Paulo itself. A further sixteen percent migrated to Brazil's largest and richest metropolitan, Greater Sao Paulo, from the neighboring South and South East regions.

Out-migration is not a new phenomenon in the North East. Rural *nordestinos*, pushed by the effects of periodic droughts and insecure land tenure situations, have been leaving the region for many decades in search of better opportunities in the cities of the South East or in the agricultural frontiers of Amazonia and the Centre West. As of 1970, some 3.5 million persons born in the North East were living elsewhere, the majority in the metropolitan areas of Sao Paulo and Rio de Janeiro. Although data released from the census are not sufficient to calculate the exact dimensions of the major migratory flows to the largest metropolitan centers in Brazil, it is possible to estimate roughly when migration occurs. The estimated rise in out-migration during the 1970s, mainly to Sao Paulo and Rio de Janeiro, is probably related to the effect of two severe droughts (1970 and 1979–80) and one partial drought (1976) which occurred during that period.

The most obvious explanation comes from analysing the composition of the "sectors" of these regions. Table 4.1 uses liberal terminology and groups the strata together into the three conventional social sectors. The largest pyramid base is again seen in the North East, followed by the South and the East. Urban and rural poverty weighs most heavily upon heads of family and upon the families themselves in these three regions. The labor market has a rudimentary level of differentiation which keeps more than 50 percent of the families in lower sector conditions. On the individual side, the most highly contrasting characteristic among the regions has to do with the education levels of the heads of families.

TABLE 4.1   Class Structure of Population by Region (%)

CLASSES	BRASILIA	RIO	SAO PAULO	SOUTH	EAST	NORTHEAST
Upper	6	6	4	3	2	1
Middle	69	62	60	39	41	33
Lower	25	32	36	58	57	66
Total	100	100	100	100	100	100

Source: Jose Pastore Inequality and Social Mobility in Brazil, University of Wisconsin Press, U.S.A., 1982.

Education

The data in Table 4.2 (Origin of Itaquera Inhabitants by Level of Education) point out clear differences in education among the various regions in Brazil. The general level of education of the inhabitants of Itaquera is higher than that of the population of Sao Paulo state. While in the latter state 18 percent of the population has a middle level of education (high school or equivalent, junior high school; or equivalent, and completed grade school) in Itaquera 65 percent of the inhabitants have a medium level of schooling. At the lower extreme of the edu-

TABLE 4.2   Origin of Itaquera Inhabitants by Level of Education %

	LOWER	MIDDLE	HIGHER	TOTAL
North East	11	18	1	30
Sao Paulo State	8	20	–	28
GSP	4	19	2	24
South East	6	6	–	12
South	1	2	–	3
Exterior	1	1	–	2
Total	31	66	3	100

Source: Processed by the author from IPI data.

No. of Respondents: 1700

cational range, the inhabitants of the COHAB housing project are above the state average, with only 31 percent as opposed to 76 percent on state level. Of the 50 percent of Itaquera's inhabitants who originate from Sao Paulo state and Greater Sao Paulo, nearly a third have a middle level of education and 2 percent higher education. If we compare the latter to the level of education of the "Nordestino" inhabitants (who represent 30 percent of the Itaquera population) we arrive at a value of 17 percent with middle range schooling (much higher than the level of education in the North East region as a whole). The finding with respect to the inhabitants of North East origin can be partially explained by the "brain drain" from the northern parts of the country to the more industrialized areas such as Sao Paulo. While statistically analysing the obtained frequencies using a chi-square test at a level of significance of 0.01, we can safely conclude that the value for chi-square equal to 110.5 signifies a strong relationship between the region of origin of Itaquera's inhabitants and their level of education.

Distribution of Income and Economic Activity

As can be shown from Table 4.3 (Area of Economic Activity of Itaquera Inhabitants by Income) more than 43 percent of the inhabitants of Itaquera have an income of 5 to 10 minimum monthly salaries while in Sao Paulo state only 25 percent belong to the latter income range. A relatively large percentage of the Itaquera population working in the industrial sector are highly paid skilled wcorkers, earning between 5 to 10 minimum salaries. Only 13 percent of the inhabitants labor force are relatively lowly paid (1–3 minimum salaries) compared to 51 percent in Sao Paulo state as a whole. The above data deviates from the Sao Paulo state income average. One should take into account that in Rio and Sao Paulo over a quarter of the workforce in manufacturing earn one minimum salary or less and over a third of workers in commerce earn one minimum salary or less, while workers earning two minimum salaries or less amount to 65 and 70 percent in the respective sectors; the situation is much worse in the North East.

Over the decade almost all workers scemed to enjoy some real increase in wages. The wages of skilled workers increased faster than those of unskilled workers. The legal minimum wage showed no discernible trend in real terms between 1970 and 1980, while the real wages of unskilled and semiskilled workers rose modestly compared to that of the more highly skilled.

At the same time the sharp rise in the price of property in the private market in recent years, especially in Sao Paulo, has increased middle sector demand for public housing. Thus, although at the initial

TABLE 4.3   Area of Economic Activity of Itaquera Inhabitants by Income (%)

Sector/Number of Monthly Salaries	1	1-2	2-3	3-4	4-5	5-7	7-10	10+	Total
Industry	1	-	3	4	8	8	12	5	41
Services	1	-	5	5	6	8	6	3	34
Social Services	-	1	3	4	4	5	4	1	22
Construction	-	-	-	-	-	1	-	-	1
Public Defence	-	-	1	-	-	-	-	-	1
Unspecified	-	-	-	-	1	-	-	-	1
Total	2	1	12	13	19	22	22	9	100

Source: Processed by the author from IPT data

No. of Respondents: 1700

planning phase COHAB intended to provide housing for low income families, the increased demand by both the public and private sectors for housing necessitated policy changes. Not only was housing allocated to groups with a higher level of income but more expensive houses were constructed (in the later construction phases of Itaquera no more houses were built for "favelados").

Of those who earn between 5 to 10 minimum salaries, 22 percent originate from the state of Sao Paulo and only 9 percent of those in the same income range originate from the North East. Although there is a tendency for educated Northeasterners to emigrate to the South East, the level of education of the former is still lower than that of Paulistas in absolute and relative terms. This is due to the small number of people in those regions able to obtain an education, especially at University level. This serves to explain the difference in levels of income. Using chi-square analysis we find a strong relation between the level of income and locality of origin.[16]

Eighty seven percent of the project's inhabitants previously lived in rented housing as opposed to 48 percent in Sao Paulo state. As to those originating from slums or who owned housing, they represent only 1 percent (in each category) of the population in Itaquera as opposed to 52 percent in Sao Paulo state. As part of the government's policy of eradication and relocation of Sao Paulo's slum dwellers, CO-HAB constructed nearly 600 small houses in Itaquera at a maximum cost of 320 upc. The latter housed favelados with less than two minimum salaries. This represented less than two percent of the total units constructed by COHAB in the east zone of the city. Although forty percent of GSP population lives in precarious shelters the municipal housing company relocated only 1 percent of the metropolitan's favelados to their largest and newest housing project.

A Concluding Note

The population of Itaquera consists mainly of inhabitants who emigrated from within the state of Sao Paulo. The second largest group emigrated from the North East region of Brazil. Both the level of education (65 percent with a middle level of education) and the level of income (43 percent earn between 5 to 10 minimum salaries) are much higher than the Sao Paulo state average. A large proportion of the population of Itaquera are employed in the tertiary sector, in the public sector (social services and public defence) and in highly skilled jobs in industry. In conclusion, according to these socioeconomic variables the population of Itaquera is hardly representative of the structural

TABLE 4.4   Level of Income of Itaquera Inhabitants by Origin

Region/Number of Monthly Salaries	Under 3	3-5	5 and Over	Total
State of Sao Paulo	5	10	15	30
North East	5	14	4	28
GSP	5	8	12	25
South East	2	3	7	12
South	–	1	2	3
Exterior	–	1	1	2
Total	17	37	46	100

Source: Processed by the author from IPT data

No. of Respondents: 1700

distribution of Sao Paulo's population. This distributional pattern indicates an urban middle sector society (see Tables 4.4 and 4.5).

It has been generally recognized that the fruits of the rapid expansion
of the Brazilian economy have been unevenly distributed. The very
success of the Brazilian growth of the late 1960s and early 1970s
produced an increase in the concentration of income, because the high
growth rates increased the demand for skilled manpower which was in
short supply. Just as market forces caused an immense rise in the
relative income of skilled laborers, technicians and managers, so a large
proportion of the increment in the real income was captured by groups
with large amounts of scarce human capital—mainly members of the
middle sectors mostly concentrated in the urbanized and heavily industrialized South East region of Brazil.

Sao Paulo, which is the main centre of economic activity and the
richest state within Brazil, is also the main area of origin of tax revenues
for the federal government. Although its housing deficit is the largest
in the nation, the level of federal expenditure on public housing is
relatively low. While the BNH attracts in Sao Paulo nearly 25 percent
of the FGTS only a mere 1 percent of the National Housing Bank's
resources are reinvested in the metropolitan area of Sao Paulo. The

TABLE 4.5 Origin of Itaquera Inhabitants by Previous Type of Housing

Region/Type of Housing	Rented	Rent-Free & Favela	Total
North East	28	2	30
State of Sao Paulo	23	5	28
GSP	22	3	25
South East	11	1	12
South	3	–	3
Exterior	1	1	2
Total	88	12	100

Source: Processed by the author from IPT data.

No. of Respondents: 1700

Paulista public housing agencies throughout its two decades of existence invested in housing programs while furthering the interests of politically dominant groups in Brazilian society. This follows the general trend of an increase in public expenditure on social services in Brazil. It seems that, although the number of units constructed by the state has increased steadily, the average cost of a public housing unit has increased dramatically. Increased demand from technocrats (both in the public and private sectors) for state provision of housing has influenced the construction policy—the building of more expensive units, but state subsidized, in the heavily urbanized South East.

As opposition parties began to win in the state elections, the government had to diversify its political strategy. Since the late 1970s, the analysis of the allocation pattern of public housing in clientelistic-patronage terminology has had increased significance. The issue of public housing became central to the political campaigns of the PDS party, especially in the interior of Sao Paulo State and the North East.

Notes

1. Christopher Clapham and George Philip, *Political Dilemmas of Military Regimes* (Kent: Croom Helm, 1985), p. 138.

2. Only in 1982 and in 1985 would the governor and the Mayor—respectively—be directly elected.

3. Antonio Carlos de Medeiros *Intergovernmental Relations in Brazil* (London School of Economics: Brazil Workshop, 1983), p. 36.

4. At the time Jorge Wilheim, who later was Director of SEMPLA during the Montoro government.

5. Antonio Carlos de Medeiros *op. cit.*, p. 42.

6. *Ibid*, p. 57.

7. *Ibid*, p. 61.

8. Richard Batley *Expansion and Exclusion in Sao Paulo—An Overview* (Sussex:Institute of Development Studies, March 1977), p. 13.

9. *Ibid.*

10. *Ibid*, p. 16.

11. *Ibid*, p. 16.

12. Gabriel Bolaffi *A Arquitectura do Poder e o Poder da Arquitectura* (Sao Paulo: Unpublished paper), 1983.

13. This part is based on interviews with COHAB staff in December 1983.

14. Gabriel Bolaffi *op. cit.*, p. 10.

15. COHAB Sao Paulo *Prezado Inscrito na Fila da COHAB*(Sao Paulo) 25/ 10/83.

16. Chi-square = 127.1; df. = 35; alpha = 0.001.

5

Non-Democratic Regimes and
Social Policy: End of an Era?

Middle Sector Beneficiaries

What can be said about the social effects of public spending in non-democratic regimes? During the 1960s and 1970s a considerable broadening of social services coverage, in the so-called Third World, coupled with an increase in government spending contributed decisively to improvement. Life expectancy at birth increased; access to potable water increased; the population per doctor declined; access to electricity increased. The share of the rural labor force decreased; the number of illiterates decreased dramatically. Nevertheless, many of the hundreds of millions of people living below the poverty threshold have yet to benefit from adequate shelter, health care and effective education. All indications are that while the expenditure by central governments on social policy increased sharply in non-democratic regimes (as well as in Western democracies), the distribution of income, which in all but a handful of nations was very skewed to begin with, did not change for the better, if at all. Why did a decade of massive domestic and international spending on social programs have so little effect?

It may help to ask who did benefit from increased public spending in social policy? It might also be possible by looking at the past scenario to predict future trends following a massive redemocratization process in the mid 1980s. Public spending undoubtedly benefited the middle sectors who were expanding at an extraordinary rate during the years preceding the debt crisis. Indeed it can be argued convincingly, that middle sector demands on non-democratic governments helped bring about the increase in social program spending which eventually proved to be inexhaustible. The middle sectors benefited in many ways from the pattern of public spending. Until the debt crisis, and in many cases even in the midst of it, government subsidies benefited mainly the middle sectors: subsidized electricity, gasoline, housing, university education and credit are heavily slanted in favor of the latter. The expansion of social security systems usually cater for the urban middle sectors rather than for the rural poor. The construction of 4-lane highways and expensive public housing are not lower class oriented projects. The expansion of public employment benefited mostly middle sectors both through income benefit and increased power vis-a-vis the state.

A key argument presented throughout this book has been that the claims by non-democratic regimes to a consistent commitment to rational, bureaucratic, or technocratic norms of government tend to be accepted at face value. For O'Donnell, with whom the development of the notion of a new "bureaucratic authoritarian" type of state is most closely associated, Brazil is the "purest" case. O'Donnell sees this type of state as a system which is "excluding" and emphatically non-democratic. Central actors in the dominant coalition include high-level technocrats—military and civilian, within and outside the state—working in close association with foreign capital. This new elite eliminates electoral competition and severely controls the political participation of the popular sector. Public policy is centrally concerned with promoting advanced industrialization. The cases of bureaucratic-authoritarianism considered by O'Donnell are the post-1964 period in Brazil, the period from 1966 to 1970 and the post-1976 period in Argentina, the post-1973 period in Chile and Uruguay and contemporary Mexico. In the case of Sao Paulo, the talk of rationality and technocracy is only partially withstanding. During the 1960s and late 1970s the military regime attempted to consolidate power on a basis other than coercion. There was an explicit commitment by the government to consolidate power by the exploitation of the monopoly of the state in key areas (e.g., housing). Political support has been won through the selective and openly partisan distribution of public housing. The present regime developed and perfected the systems of patronage and clientelism, instead of eliminating the "corrupt" sytems of the civilian politicians. During this period public housing was not only a highly politicized issue at national levels but also at the regional level.

The vast academic literature dealing with different aspects of politics in non-democratic regimes has given little thought to the analysis of military regimes, politics and the implementation of social policies. I have tried to argue here that the ability of long-term non-democratic regimes to control the economy was not only through the imposition of force but mainly through political manipulation. Staying in power for such a long period requires the military to look for fairly long-term sources of political support, which invariably involves it in some kind of clientelist strategy, to control state resources and buy support. Such a clientelist system operates not only on the military's terms but also depends on the direct influence of the technocrats as the state apparatus cannot be totally autonomous or isolated from the latter. It is in the development and management of public housing that we see most clearly the extension and diffusion of bureaucratic power. In all Third World countries housing is the most pressing problem and many studies reveal how in situations of great scarcity even the "first-line bureaucrats" acquire the capacity to affect decisions concerning applications and allocations. It is often the case that discretionary control over access to public goods lies in the hands, not of the top policy-making bureaucrats, but of the lower echelons in the system.

The construction of "pharaonic" projects, such as nuclear power stations, large hydro-electric projects, urban underground transport and large scale housing projects in the 1960s and late 1970s, was widely used in government propaganda throughout various non-democratic regimes. The new 5000 kilometre TransAmazonica highway, for example, was presented as a fearless, patriotic undertaking carried out by a government in a hurry to develop the hinterland and to bring progress to the poorest sectors of the population. The construction of a large number of low quality housing units in the North East region of Brazil was used with some success to divert attention away from the violent political repression of that time and to present the military administrations as effective governments which were rapidly developing the country. A similar case can be seen in the construction of the Aswan dam in Egypt.

The increased visibility of political corruption has become a persistent and disturbing feature of non-democratic societies. Behaviour that will be considered corrupt is likely to be more prominent in less developed countries because of a variety of conditions involved in their underdevelopment: greater inequality in distribution of wealth, political office as the primary means of gaining access to wealth, conflict between changing moral codes, the weakness of social and government enforcement mechanisms, the absence of a strong sense of national community and the weakness of the legitimacy of governmental institutions.[1] In furthering the interests of politically dominant social groups, public enterprises are frequently used as instruments for these aims. Thus the state corporation, CODESPAULO, was managed mainly by PDS members who supported Paulo Salim Maluf. Public enterprises can easily become means of patronage whereby support is bought, and this can take forms ranging from the decision to establish them and their location to the offers of important posts. Patronage is a controversial technique. An appointment to one of the many public housing agencies may be used to influence the attitudes and values of some citizens, or reward people for supporting the regime or government. But patronage can be interpreted more widely and can go beyond these examples, in that quite junior public officials can effectively decide who obtains or benefits from public policy products. It is not suprising that inefficiency and corruption prevail in the Brazilian public housing sector. Even when management autonomy is allowed in such agencies as CODES-PAULO, it has no meaning unless it can be exercised well and responsibly. In many non-democratic regimes, however, neither management systems nor managers were available to assure competent and responsible administration of public enterprises. Under such circumstances, occurrences of failure in performance and of corruption will be found in the public sector. Too many government corporations were set up by state, federal and municipal governments without taking responsible action to assure the support of management capabilities. Non-democratic regimes in Third World countries tend to display a high level of autonomy. At the same time, state power—despite the impressive use of force which is frequently displayed—is fragile and Praetorian politics are the norm. In part this political instability is due to a series of fairly rapid shifts in the development models being pursued.[2] The failure of the regime to manage economic policy, as has been the case since 1973, has undermined the post-1964 governments' attempts to justify authoritarian measures on the grounds of efficiency. Even the regime's main source of civilian support, the business community and the urban sectors, came to believe that failure of the government to manage the economy was caused by the special favours granted to state companies controlled by the military. Extreme right factions of the armed forces threatened Geisel and Golbery's project of political "decompression." The hard-liner groups within the military began to eradicate the bases of left-wing organizations. Political leaders such as General Golbery ended these human rights abuses, as they feared their own political positions would be undermined by these same groups. During this era the hard-liners began to realize that unless a new strategy was adopted, the authority of the ruling party would be undermined.

In the November 1974 election of federal deputies, the government party held on to a greatly reduced lead. In part this turnabout at the elections had to do with the growing disaffection of the population in the large urban centers. Although the most obvious solution to the deteriorating electoral fortunes of ARENA might have seemed simple: by putting a stop to the elections, the military regime began to look for ways of maintaining itself in office by changing the rules of the game. The adoption of a clientelistic approach throughout the political and administrative system has effectively channelled and scaled down demands and paralysed nearly all potential opposition. In the elections of April 1977 and 1979 the government used a classic way of making popular support effective: electoral engineering. This enabled the regime to provide itself with at least some appearance of popular support.

As we have seen in previous chapters the control of the state carries with it the power to allocate benefits in the forms of jobs and public resources (e.g., housing, education, health and social security). The delivery of benefits, in the form of economic allocations from the centre to the constituency, or of a personal pay-off, provides military regimes with political support. The regime then, was never more than partially "bureaucratic". On the basis of these arguments it is possible to conclude that elements from the Neo-Marxist and Patronage Clientelist theories help to explain these key findings. Finally, let us go back to the beginning and ask why in an authoritarian regime did politics have such an important influence on the allocation of social program resources? One answer lies in the importance of elite politics as is seen in the most important (both politically and economically) state in Brazil. As early as the Old Republic, Sao Paulo presented features of elite politics. From 1932 onwards there have been attempts to undermine Sao Paulo's political force although not always with great success. The whole question of the choice of state governors, such as Abreu Sodre, Laudo Natel, Paulo Egydio Martins, Paulo Maluf and Franco Montorro, provides a microcosm of Sao Paulo elite politics and its intertwining with national politics, through both civilians and military officers. This "Sao Paulo" connection was of vital importance as it has always been in modern Brazilian politics. All these Paulista governors were deeply involved in civilian-military politics and the contending economy.

The distribution of resources for the construction of public housing in Sao Paulo has been regressive and politics has been a significant factor to this regressivity. During periods when the pro-government party (ARENA) was in power, the governorship of Sao Paulo was directed to the centre (1967–79) and especially when the Paulista elites had a direct link with the centre through the Finance minister—Delfim Netto—a vast proportion of public housing resources were allocated to Sao Paulo (as the cost per unit is the highest in Brazil). The large-scale projects, Itaquera and St. Etelvina, show that Sao Paulo got better quality housing but for more up-market groups of recipients than the North East region.

Since the pro-government faction of the PDS lost its majority to the supporters of Paulo Maluf, less resources have been transferred by the BNH to Sao Paulo state. The 1982 elections in Sao Paulo confirmed a pattern which was already clear in 1974: an overt hostility towards the national regime coupled with an increase of party politics. As the PMDB won the state governorship elections in 1982, even less federal funds were allocated to finance public housing. But the latter is only one factor influencing the Paulista housing market. Another is the bureaucracy's ideological and cultural bias. Yet another can be attributed to political corruption. And the fourth: the purchasing power of the urban sectors. During the boom years most of the demand by the latter for housing was supplied by the private construction firms. It was during the periods of economic crisis (mid 1970s till early 1980s) as the tripling of oil prices put an end to the "miracle" that the public housing agencies (COHABS, INOCOOPS and CODESPAULO) began to construct vast numbers of housing units in the large urban centers, as the middle sectors could not afford to purchase dwellings from the private market.

To conclude, it appears that the vast academic literature on social policy in Brazil has overlooked a number of important and increasingly central features. It is not suprising to discover that politics was a contributing factor to inequality in a semi-open political system (1964–66 and during the late 1970s). As the military regime was not really authoritarian it tried to win political support by co-opting the middle sectors. This co-optation was unsuccessful during the Lacerda period but had limited success during the Paulo Maluf governorship (late 1970s to early 1980s). In these two cases, Lacerda and Paulo Maluf, this co-optation of the middle sectors came into conflict with the bureaucratic authoritarian regime. This led to dictatorship in 1966 and to democracy in the 1980s. One of the paradoxes of politics under the military regime in Brazil has been the degree to which State-directed political clientelism and, some might argue, state-directed political corruption, has increased rather than withered under a self-styled "modernising" regime.

Thus, it remains to be seen how social policy will fare under a new civilian government, but it is unlikely that political factors will lessen in importance. Finally let us go back to the beginning and ask why do non-democratic regimes subsidise social goods? Social programs are essential because of technocratic necessity; because they further the development of the welfare state; because of their capacity for creating employment; as a way to co-opt the middle sectors; and because of the ideological and cultural bias of the bureaucracy.

International Aid Organizations and Social Policy

Three decades ago, 20 percent of the population in developing countries lived in urban areas. Twenty years ago this proportion had reached

31 percent. By the year 2000 it will be 45 percent. Furthermore, the large metropolises are growing at a faster pace. Since Sub-Saharan African states gained their independence, many of their cities have increased more than sevenfold. Metropolitan centres such as Mexico City, Sao Paulo, Manila, Jakarta, Khartoum and Bogota have tripled or quadrupled their populations. One of the major problems facing such cities is the large-scale deprivation and unmet welfare services housing, employment, education, health and transportation needs. While it is true that those countries which are loosely referred to as the Third World have made much progress over the last few decades, government and international involvement in the provision of social goods is a relatively recent development.

International aid agencies and national politicians often find it difficult to agree on the necessary public policies and planning actions to cope with this dramatic increase in Third World urbanization. Despite this lack of agreement, it was possible to see in the 1970s a new international initiative which recognised the problems of the Third World cities; urban lending and technical assistance programs by multilateral financial agencies, chief among them the World Bank. Urban lending, which focuses on four types of projects (shelter, transport, integrated and regional), is a recent departure in the World Bank practice. Robert McNamara, President from 1968 to 1981, was the initiator in the direct involvement of a lending institution in social programs aimed at attacking "absolute poverty" in both urban and rural areas. The strategic point of entry into the urban scene was the financing of shelter for the lower sectors of the population. During the decade 1972–82 the Bank lent US$ 2014 million for 62 urban projects in various developing countries. Shelter projects accounted for more than half the projects supported. The Bank emphasized a shift from the construction of public housing, which was expensive to construct and maintain, to shelter projects designed at lower standards affordable to the poor, recoverable in terms of costs, and therefore replicable on a larger scale (e.g., sites and services schemes). This raises the question of why non-democratic regimes were party to these projects in the first place. Undertaking poverty-oriented projects in countries with a military regime seems contrary to their political systems and economic development strategies. One possible reason why a country might implement such projects is that military regimes wished to give a symbolic gesture in the direction of reform. Another reason why a non-democratic government undertook such poverty-oriented projects is, ironically, the possibilty that the latter might actually serve to consolidate authoritarian regimes.

As the World Bank entered its second decade of lending for social development projects in non-democratic regimes there remains the question about its continued effectiveness and relevance. The Bank's shift in the late 1970s and early 1980s from its traditional "retailer" role to "wholesaler" in urban development finance re-emphasized the definition of their goals in sound business terms such as affordability, cost recovery and replicability. This meant a marked shift from lending for specific projects to lending directly to strengthen government-created institutions. Direct loans to the BNH enabled the Brazilian military government to build houses which would meet the demands of the middle sectors.

A number of changes, varying in degree of feasibility, could conceivably improve the the Bank's future effectiveness as an antipoverty instrument. More urban social aid is necessary and a higher priority should be given to the requirements of funding grassroots activities. The Bank might also consider joint venture funding with other development assistance agencies, particularly those largely devoted to antipoverty work. The Bank should also encourage the expansion of private voluntary organizations in developing countries. The mid 1980s signals the end of an era; one which began with a crusade against poverty and concludes with a growing emphasis on changing economic policy (which usually means encouraging devaluation and liberalizing trade).

Redemocratization and Social Policy:
A Challenge for Civilian Governments

Among the new states of Africa, Asia, and Latin America, no political question has been more central, controversial, and enduring than the possibility of democratic government. The 1980s has been a decade of rapidly accelerating democratization in Southern Europe and Latin America and one of rising pressures for democratization in Asia and Africa. Throughout the two former regions there have emerged formal, constitutional democracies, laden with relatively honest and open elections, active party competition, and a comparatively uncensored press. Currently the fashionable word in Third World studies is "redemocratization." A brief glance at the political structures now in place across the South American continent suffices to understand why.

While in 1979, fourteen of the twenty countries on the Latin American mainland, between the Rio Grande and Tierra de Fuego, were ruled by military governments, as of early 1986, only two of those fourteen continue to have military regimes, Pinochet's Chile and Stroessner's Paraguay. Between 1982 and 1985, civilian regimes were established, for very different reasons and through dissimilar processes, in Argentina, Brazil and Uruguay. Peru, with the election of Alan Garcia in 1985, consolidated that process. The most long-standing democracies, Colombia and Venezuela, reinforced that tradition. In retrospect, the first half of the 1980s might well prove to have been a significant quinquennium in Latin American politics, though it is strongly advised to use the word "might" given the unpredictability of the South American continent. In an attempt to grapple with the important question: "Is the return to democracy permanent or is is it part of a cycle of military and civilian regimes?" a vast number of books and articles have been written both by Western and Latin American academics.

Such political developments coincided, more or less, with an economic depression for the entire continent for which, in this century, only the Great Depression of 1929–31 invites comparison. Its causes were complex and its outcome still remains, for the vast majority of states, uncertain. All the new democratic regimes inherited from their military predecessors enormous economic problems, in which the size of the external debt was a major factor. The new literature on redemocratization subsumes at least three different theoretical problems: Why do authoritarian regimes break down? What are the different paths of transition to which they may give rise? What factors determine the success of democratic consolidation? The literature tries to answer these three theoretical controversies while acknowledging that ideally the study of democratization should begin with the study of authoritarianism. The reasons which explain the pattern established in non-democratic regimes of deepening economic recession, coupled with national and international opposition to dictatorship, culminating in a transition to democracy are rather complex. Taken together the literature discusses economic, political, and cultural aspects which led to the crisis, from different disciplinary perspectives and theoretical orientations. A central point which this literature seems to have missed is that the present movement by civilian interests away from authoritarianism springs mainly from the exclusionary tendency of these regimes. In the end, access to power and control over distributable goods is the name of the game, not forms of regimes. Parties in non-democratic regimes historically have not been the main vehicle for representing civil society to the state and thereby providing an ongoing infrastructural link between state and society that can legitimate specific regime types.

Although this institutional structural problem has many sources, a major one is the predisposition of these societies towards a patrimonial social structure. They are formed around diffuse vertical hierarchies that link central structure to the people by means of ascending and descending patron-client ties. This deep structural tendency helps account for the fact that while class and interest-group dynamics exist in these societies, they are often overridden or blunted by vertical cross-class and status-group clientelistic dynamics.[3] This underlying dynamic has a number of politically relevant consequences. The first is that key groups look to the state as the patrimonial source of privileges. Group strategy is used mainly to directly penetrate the state through the executive apparatus to extract specific concessions. Parties and legislatures are not the preferred vehicle for interest representation. Rather, the inclination is to capture executive sources of benefits that flow more as patronage and privileges than as universal rights. Most groups and factional leaders have shown over and over again that the main issue for them is access to the executive lodestone and not formalized democratic procedures of rule-making and conflict resolution.

The past record would indicate then, that many groups, parties, and factions support a return to democracy not out of a primary commitment to liberal government, but as a result of concrete negative experience with the alternative. For the last two decades non-democratic regimes acted in an exclusionary manner. The state's forceful exclusion of the lower sector of society was all too obvious. However, many of these regimes also acted as closed circles of military and technocratic decision makers that denied regularized channels of access to other groups as well. Hence, many groups that originally supported the non-democratic regimes turned against them because of the erratic patterns of access offered to them and the impact upon them of social and economic policies that were formed with little or no counsel from them. Party leaders as well as some leaders of other social groups (e.g., technocrats), even when they were formally identified with the regime, have pressured the regime to "decompress" so as to open more access to patronage. Thus, if democracy in contemporary Latin America and Southern Europe is to prevail, governments must distribute social and economic benefits to all key players. Moreover, ways must be found to convert electoral and legislative action into channels of access to power such that legislatures, elections, and parties can articulate and represent interests of civil society.

Finally, one might ask how far this book indicates the direction which non-democratic regimes are likely to take in the future. In discussing both the factors that hinder and the ones that contribute to the process of democratization it is possible to identify three negative factors: the economic crisis, the fact that in several of the large South American countries the institutional basis of authoritarianism and corporatism is still in place, and finally a weak tradition of liberal-democratic regimes. The favorable factors are: the de-legitimation of authoritarian non-democratic forms of governance as a consequence of their failure, and the commitment by the new civilian administrations to institutionalize the two most important dimensions of democracy, participation and contestation.

Has Social Policy a Future?

We began by looking at the trends of an increasing expenditure on social policy programs in non-democratic regimes and explained why the situation is similar to that of Western democracies. Evidence from Brazil shown throughout the book illustrates that the middle sectors were the main beneficiaries of increased public spending during the two decades of military rule. The fundamental question is that with demands for social policy services constantly rising during an era of heavy debt service obligations in the face of depressed commodity markets and a great scarcity of external capital, how should governments reform their social programs in order to benefit the most vulnerable groups in society? This fundamental question aside, what else is important for consideration? Obviously, it is important to relate the former question vis-a-vis the redemocratization process. What then of the future of social policy that represents the interests of the middle sectors? We shall do our best to answer these questions in the light of the material presented in the earlier chapters.

First, consider the alternatives. Essentially they seem to be either a return to free market, or a socialist revolution. Let us look at each briefly. The free-market option is currently being tried in Britain and the United States. Its logic is economic and social laissez-faire. The expansion of government-controlled industries, social services and agencies in non-democratic regimes, has imposed a fiscal burden on the economy. The current attention being focused on the free market option in the context of developing countries is essentially a phenomenon of the mid-1980s, and has been fuelled by the example of the privatization and de-regulation programs adopted in a number of industrial countries (notably the United Kingdom and the United States). The term "privatization" is used to describe a range of different policy initiatives designed to alter the balance between the public and private sectors. We will distinguish between three main approaches to privatization. The first and most common usage of the term refers to a change in the ownership of an enterprise (or part of an enterprise) from the public to the private sector. A second mode of privatization involves the liberalisation, or deregulation, of entry into activities previously restricted to public sector enterprises. The third sense in which the word privatization has been used is when the provision of a good or a service is transferred from the public to private sector, while the government retains ultimate responsibility for supplying the service.[4]

Those who are currently making the case for greater privatization in housing (in Western democracies) argue that its attributes, its methods of production and allocation, and its value to the individual consumer and the community make it far more suitable for organization by the market than has been accepted by policy-makers over the last decades. The ideological viewpoint behind this statement is that private incentives induce efficiency and consumer orientation, while the public sector tends to be dominated by the interest of suppliers, managers and local politicians. Market discipline, in other words, is likely to be more effective than public influence, and the lack of such discipline is likely to result in an organizational slack. Private production and allocation together with state subsidy are therefore seen as a more effective way of meeting housing requirements than is direct provision. Yet, when one looks at what little evidence there is on the relative efficiency of the two sectors, the position is by no means straightforward.[5]

Privatization has been extensively debated as a policy option in many non-democratic regimes and a number of countries have already implemented privatization measures. Despite the vast number of examples of privatization programs, the overall picture is that so far only limited divesture has taken place in non-democratic regimes (excluding Chile). Because of rudimentary or non-existent capital markets in non-democratic countries, a recent study estimated that most privatized firms were small in terms of asset value and employment, and had been previously in private ownership.[6] A second sense of privatization, deregulation, has been widely used in non-democratic regimes not least because international aid agencies (e.g., World Bank and IMF) have increasingly attached it as an important element in the conditionality of lending programs to public enterprises. The question remains if in the foreseeable future this mode of privatization will be applied by the latter agencies to social policy programs. In a sense deregulation, or liberalization, has been applied in several non-democratic regimes. The removal of restrictions on market entry is intended to increase the role of competition. A recent study has shown that the role of the private sector is pervasive in the provision of services in developing countries. To support the latter argument the study describes dozens of examples of so-called public services in education, health, electricity, urban transport, telecommunications and water supply that are in fact being privately provided in more than fifty developing countries.[7]

Although the examples of deregulation are vast, analysis of this type of privatization policy is lacking. The argument in this section on privatization can be summarised as follows. Improvements in economic performance of social policy agencies (e.g., COHAB, CODESPAULO, INOCOOP) are more likely to result from an increase in market competition than from a change from public to private ownership. The lack of competition of housing aimed at middle sector segments of the urban population during periods of economic crisis (for the middle sectors) not only reduced the economic performance of state housing agencies but also resulted in the politicization of the distribution process. It is likely that increased competition will also reduce the "patron-client" character of the allocation of social resources. Not only competition between the private and public sectors but also increased competition between state and municipal and trade union housing agencies. The current situation is that COHAB, CODESPAULO and INOCOOP are not competing with each other but rather each agency has a separate segment of the housing market. There are important constraints, however, on increasing competition in non-democratic regimes. Where state monopolies dominate that market, the removal of statutory barriers to entry will be insufficient to stimulate competiton, and regulatory agencies will have to be established to control the behaviour of the privatized enterprises.[8]

The third sense in which the term privatization has been used, franchising or contracting-out of public services and the leasing of public assets to the private sector, is again an area where analysis in the context of non-democratic regimes is lacking. Although state and municipal agencies in the area of housing provision have a relatively long tradition of contracting-out certain services (e.g., in the field of architecture, new building, improvement, repair and maintenance, urban planning) it is obvious that a further reduction in the services provided by these agencies and the amplification of the tendering process to other social sectors (e.g., health, education) could result in massive anti-privatization campaigns. Furthermore, there is no evidence from non-democratic regimes that suggests that the private sector is relatively more efficient than the public sector in for example constructing new buildings, or in improving, repairing or in the maintenance of existing housing stock.

What of the socialist alternative? The return of the military to the "barracks" in the mid-1980s in many non-democratic regimes, notably in Latin America, does not by any means signify radical changes in social policy. Although we might also have expected the civilian governments not only to increase the allocation of resources to social programs but also to redistribute to lower income sectors such expectations are unlikely to be realised. It is also important to remind ourselves of the limits—or rather the limitations—of a socialist alternative. The impact of the post-1980 economic crisis on social sectors in non-democratic regimes has been very severe. Public expenditure on social sectors has been cut down by budgetary constraints at federal level and probably also reduced at state and local government levels. Although we would have expected a sharp decrease in the military budget during an era when the soldiers have recently returned to the barracks, this is not the situation (except in Argentina). In Brazil and Spain the military fared better as a budgetary pressure group under a democratic government and the defense budget percentage of GNP rose somewhat. Civilian politicians, faced with a series of economic and political crises, have tended to transfer education, health and housing services from the jurisdiction of the central government to that of provincial governments wihout corresponding resources, leaving the poorer provinces at the mercy of the central government's transfers and thus making long-term planning of services nearly impossible. In short, both the effectiveness and rational-comprehensive nature of the social planning processes in non-democratic regimes are in jeopardy. Even in the new democracies it seems as if intensifying political pressure will predominate in the planning process.

Notes

1. A. Heidenheimer, *Political Corruption* (USA: Holt and Rinehart, 1970), p. 4.

2. Ian Roxborough, *Theories of Underdevelopment* (UK: Macmillan, 1979), p. 123–124.

3. David Chalmers, "Parties and Society in Latin America", in Steffen Schmidt et al. *Friends, Followers and Clients* (Berkley and Los Angeles: University of California Press, 1977), pp. 401–21.

4. See: Paul Cook and Colin Kirkpatrick, *Privatisation in Less Developed Countries* (Sussex: Wheatsheaf Books, 1988).

5. Christine Whitehead, "Privatisation and Housing", in Julian Le Grand and Ray Robinson *Privatisation and the Welfare State* (London: George Allen & Unwin, 1985), pp. 116–132.

6. Paul Cook, *Privatisation*, pp. 28–29.

7. Gabriel Roth, *The Private Provision of Public Services in Developing Countries* (USA: Oxford University Press, 1987).

8. Paul Cook, *Privatisation*, p. 27.

Bibliography

Books and Articles

Aaron, Henry. *Shelter and Subsidies: Who Benefits from Federal Housing Policies?* Washington: Brooking Institution, 1972.

Abercrombie, Nicholas, and Urry, J. *Capital, Labour & the Middle Classes.* London: Allen & Unwin, 1983.

Aguiar, Marco Antonio de Souza, and Arruda M., and Flores, P. *Ditadura Economica Versus Democracia.* Rio de Janeiro: BASE Editora Codecri, 1983.

Albrow, Martin. *Bureaucarcy—Key Concepts in Political Science.* London: Pahl Mall, 1970.

Allen, Gilbert. *Latin American Development.* London: Penguin, 1977.

Allison, Graham. *Essence of Decision: Explaining the Cuban Missile Crisis.* USA.: Little Brown & Co., 1971.

Almeida, Wanderly de, and Chautard, Jose, L, *FGTS: Uma Politica de Bem Estar Social.* Rio de Janeiro: IPEA, 1976.

Almond, G. and Colman. *The Politics of the Developing Areas.* N.J.: Princeton UP, 1960.

Alves, Maria Helena. "Grassroots Organizations, Trade Unions, and the Church: A Challenge to the Controlled Abertura in Brazil" in *Latin American Perspectives.* Issue No. 40 , Vol. No. 1, Winter 1984.

_____ . *Estado e Oposicao no Brasil.* Petropolis: Vozes, 1984.

Ames, Barry. "Rhetoric and Reality in a Military Regime: Brazil since 1964" in A. Lowethal (ed). *The Armies and Politics of Latin America.* USA: Holmes & Meir, 1977.

Andrade, Luis Aureliano de. "Politica Urbana do Brasil: O Paradigma A Organizacao E A Politica " *Estudos CEBRAP.* No. 18, Oct, 1976.

Ascher, W. *Scheming for the Poor: the Politics of Redistribution in Latin America.* Boston: Harvard UP, 1984.

Associacao Brasilera de COHABs, *Habitacao Popular* Rio de Janeiro, June 1983.

Azevedo, Sergio de. "Politica de Habitacoo Popular: Balanco e Prespectiva" *Dados* Publicacao do Instituto Universitario de Pesquisas do Rio de Janeiro, No. 22, 1979, pp. 99–118.

_____ . *A Politica Habitacional Para As Classes de Baixa Renda.* (Tese de Mestrado), Rio: IUPERJ, 1975.

_____ , and Andrade, Luis, Aureliano, Gama de. *Habitacao e Poder.* Brazil: Zahar Editores, 1982.

Baer, Werner. *The Brazilian Economy: Growth & Development.* USA: Praeger, Second Edition, 1983.

Ball, Michael. *Housing Policy & Economic Power.* London: Metheun, 1983.

Banco Nacional de Habitacao, *Relatorios,* Rio de Janeiro.

———, *Instrucoes as COHABs,* Rio de Janeiro, No. 63, 14/4/1966.

———, *Documento de Orientacao aos Dirigentes de COHABs,* Rio de Janeiro, 1982.

———, *Legislacao Basica do BNH,* Rio de Janeiro, 1979.

Barros, Mario.*A Fantastica Corrupcao No Brasil.* Sao Paulo: Edicao do Autor, 1982.

Batley, Richard.*Power Through Bureaucracy: Urban Political Analysis in Brazil* UK: Gower, 1983.

———. "Urban Renewal and Expulsion in Sao Paulo" in Gilbert, and Hardoy, and Ramirez. *Urbanization in Contemporary Latin America.* UK: John Wiley, 1982, pp. 231–262.

———."Urban Politics and Bureaucracy in Brazil" in *Public Administration Bulletin* 1981, pp. 14–35.

———. "The Allocation of Public Contracts: Studies in Peru and Venezuela"in *Development and Change.* Vol. 11, 1980, pp. 211–227.

———. *BNH: Establishment and Adaptation.*Birmingham: D.A.G. Occasional Paper No 5, Nov. 1979.

———. *Expansion & Exclusion in Sao Paulo—An Overview.* IDS, March, 1977.

Baumol, William, "Macro-economics of Unbalanced Growth: The Autonomy of Urban Crisis" in Heilbroner, and Ford. *Is Economics Relevant?* California: Goodyear Publishing Co., 1971, pp. 108–118

Blay, Eva, Alterman. *A Luta Pelo Espaco.* Petropolis: Editora Vozes, 1978.

Boddy, Martin, and Gray, Fred. "Filtering Theory, Housing Policy and the Legitimation of Inequality", in *Policy and Politics.* Vol.7, 1979, pp. 39–54.

Bolaffi, Gabriel. "A Casa das Illusoes Perdidas" in *Cadernos CEBRAP.* 27, Ed. Brasiliense, 1977.

———."Urban Land Policy in Brazil" in *Habitat International.* Vol. 41, No. 45, 1980, pp. 581–591.

———. "A Questao Urbana: Producao de Habitacao, Construcao Civil e Mercado de Trabalho" *Novos Estudos CEBRAP.* Vol. 2, No. 1, Abril 1983, pp. 61–68

———. "Planejamento Urbano: Reflexao Sobre a Experienca Recente" *Novos Estudos CEBRAP.* Vol. 1, No. 41, Nov. 1982.

———. "Habitacao e Urbanismo: O Problema e O Falso Problema", in Maricato E. *A Producao Capitalista de Casas e da Cidade no Brasil Industrial.* Sao Paulo: Alfa Omega, 1979, pp. 37–70.

———. *A Arquitectura do Poder e o Poder da Arquitectura.* Sao Paulo: Unpublished Paper, Dec/1983.

Bondukie, Nabil, George. "Origens do Problema da Habitacao Popular En Sao Paulo—Primeiros Estudos" *Espaco e Debates—Revista de Estudos Regional e Urbanos.* Marco/Junho 1982, pp. 81–111

———, and Rolnik, R. *Periferias: Ocupacao do Espaco e Reproducao da Forca de Trabalho.* Sao Paulo: FAU–USP, 1979.

Bowen, Elinor. "The Pressman–Wildavsky Paradox", in *Journal of Public Policy.* Vol. 2, Part 1, Feb. 1982, pp. 1–21.

Brandao, Maria de Azevedo. "O Engenho da Producao: Limites da Producao Habitacional de Interesse Social no Brasil" in *Cadernos do CEAS.* No. 87, Setembro/Outobro 1983, pp. 8–25.

Brasiliero, Ana Maria. " O 'Elitismo" da Legislacao Urbanistica" *Revista de Administracao Municipal.* No. 147, Abril/Junho 1978, pp. 7–15.

Bremaeker, Francois. "Urbanizacao em Marcha" *Revista de Administracao Municipal.* No. 166, Jan/Marco 1983, pp. 60–90.

_____ . "As Regioes Metropolitanas em Processo de Superconcentracao Populacional" *Revista de Administracao Municipal.* No. 164, Jul/Set 1982, pp. 68–81

Brigagao, Clovis. *A Militarizacao da Sociedade.*Rio: JZE, 1985.

Brown, R.G.S., and Steel, D. *The Administrative Process in Britain.* UK: Metheun, 1979.

Bunker, Stephen. "Policy Implementation in an Authoritarian State: A Case from Brazil" in *Latin American Research Review.* Vol. XVIII, No. 1. 1983, pp. 33–59.

Butterworth, Douglas, and Chance, J. *Latin American Urbanization.* USA: CUP, 1981.

Burgess, Rod. "The Politics of Urban Residence in Latin America" in *International Journal of Urban & Regional Research.* Vol. 6, No. 4, 1982, pp. 465–480.

_____ . "Ideology and Urban Residential Theory in Latin America" in Herbert, D., and Johnston (eds). *Geography and Urban Environment.* Vol. IV, USA: John Wiley, 1981, Ch. 3, pp. 57–114.

Camargo, Candido de. (ed). *Sao Paulo: 1975—Crescimento e Pobreza.* Sao Paulo: Edicoes Loyola, 1982.

Camargo, Elias. "O Desenvolvimento das Favelas Na Grande Sao Paulo" *Problemas Brasileiros: Revista Mensal de Cultura.* No. 223, Maio 1983, pp. 7–14.

Camargo, Nelly, and Noya Pinto, V. *Communication Policy in Brazil.*Paris: UNESCO Press, 1975.

Cammack, Paul. "Bureaucratic-Authoritarianism: a Dissenting Note" *Politics.* Vol. 2, No. 1, April 1982.

_____ . "Clientelism and Military Government in Brazil" Clapham, C. *Private Patronage and Public Power: Political Clientelism in the Modern State.* UK: Frances Pinter, 1982.

Campos, Roberto. "A Retrospect Over Brazilian Developments Plans" in Howard, E. (ed). *The Economy of Brazil.* USA: University of California Press, 1969, Ch. 11

Canak, W. "The Peripheral State Debate: State Capitalist & Bureaucratic-Authoritarian Regimes in Latin America" in *Latin American Research Review.* Vol. XIX, No. 1, 1984.

Cardoso, H. *Autoritarismo e Democraticazao.* Brazil: Paz e Terra, 1975.

_____ . "Sao Paulo e Seus Problemas Sociais" in *CEBRAP.* No. 14, 1973, pp. 91–99.

_____ . "Dependency & Development in Latin America" *NLR*. July/August 1972.

_____ , and Faletto, E. *Dependencia y Desarrollo en America Latina*. Chile: 1967.

Castells, Manuel. *The Urban Question*. London: Edward Arnold, 1977.

_____ . *City, Class & Power*. London: Macmillan, 1978.

_____ , and Godard, F. *Monopoville*. Paris: Mouton, 1974.

_____ , and Murray, D., and Potter, and Politt, C. (editors) *Decisions, Organizations & Society*. UK: Penguin Books, 1978.

Castro, Antonio Barros de. *A Economia Brasileira em Marcha Forcada*. Rio: Paz e Terra, 1985.

Castro, I. E. de. "Conjunto Habitacional Ampliando a Controversia Sobre a Remocao de Favelas" in *DADOS: Revista de Ciencas Sociais*. Vol. 26., No. 2, 1982.

Chaloult, Yves. *Estado, Acumulacao e Colonialismo Interno*. Brasil: Vozes, 1978.

Clapham, Christopher. *Third World Politics*. London: Croom Helm, 1985.

Cleaves, Peter. *Bureaucratic Politics and Administration in Chile*. USA: University of California Press, 1974.

Colletti, Lucio. (ed). *Karl Marx: Early Writings*. UK: Harmondsworth, Penguin Books, 1975.

Collier, D. (ed). *The New Authoritarianism in Latin America*. Princeton UP, 1979.

_____ . *Squatters & Oligarchs: Authoritarian Rule and Policy Change in Peru*. John Hopkins University Press, 1976.

Coutinho, L., "Administracao Decentralizada em Sao Paulo" in *Revista de Administracao de Empresas*. RJ: Junio, 1979.

Crevenna, T. (ed). *Materiales para el Estudio de las Classes Medias en America*. Washington: Union Panamericana, 1952.

Currie, Lauchlin. "Housing as an Instrument of Macro–Economic Policy" in *Habitat International*. Vol. 7, No. 5/6, 1983, pp. 165–171.

Dahrendorf, R. *Class and Class Conflict in Industrial Society*. London: 1959.

Daland, Robert. *Brazilian Planning: Development Politics and Administration*. Chapel Hill: University of North Carolina Press, 1967.

Dickens, Peter, Duncan, and Goodwin, M, and Gray. *Housing, States and Localities*. London: Methuen, 1985.

Drakakis–Smith, David. *High Society: Housing Provision in Hong Kong, 1954– 1979*. University of Hong Kong, Centre of Asian Studies, 1979.

_____ . "Low-Cost Housing Provision in the Third World: Some Theoretical & Practical Alternatives" in Murison, H. S., and Lea, J. *Housing in the Third World Countries*. London: Macmillan Press, 1979.

Dye, D.R., and Souza e Silva, C. "A Perspective on the Brazilian State" in *Latin American Research Review*. Vol. XIV, No. 1, 1979, pp. 81–98.

Dunleavy, P. *The Politics of Mass Housing in Britain: 1945–1975*. Oxford: Claredon Press, 1981.

_____ . *Urban Political Analysis*. London: Macmillan Press, 1980.

Engels, F. *The Origins of the Family, Private Property and the State.* London: Lawrence & Wishart, 1972.

Etzioni, Amitai. *Modern Organizations.* New Jersey: Prentice Hall, 1964.

Evans, Peters. *Dependent Development.* USA: Princeton, 1979.

Fesler, J.. *Public Administration—Theory and Practice.* New Jersey: Prentice-Hall, 1980.

Fiechter, Georges-Andre. *Brazil Since 1964.* UK: Macmillan Press, 1975.

Finer, S.E. *The Man on Horseback.* Penguin, 1975.

Fleisher, D. "1978: Eleicoes Parlamentares Sob A Egidedo Pacote de Brasil" *Revista de Ciencia Politica.* S.P.: Vol. 23, No. 2, Aug/1980, pp. 56–82.

_____. "O Pluripartidarismo No Brasil" in *Revista de Cienca Politica.* No. 1, Ab/1981, p. 49

Flyn, Peter. *Brazil—A Political Analysis.* UK: E. Benn, 1978.

Frank, A.G. *Capitalism and Underdevelopment in Latin America.* Penguin, 1970.

Furtado, Celso. *Economic Development of Latin America.* London: CUP, 1976.

Furtado, C. *Formacao Economica do Brasil.* S.P.: Editora Nacional, 1971.

_____. *No to Recession & Unemployment.* London: Third World Foundation, 1984.

Gilbert, A. "Bogota", in Pacione, M. (ed). *Problems and Planning in Third World Cities.* London: Croom Helm, 1981, pp. 65–93.

_____. and Gugler, J. *Cities, Poverty and Development.* UK: OUP, 1982.

_____. and Ward, P. "Public Intervention, Housing and Land Use in Latin American Cities" in *Bulletin of Latin American Studies.* Vol. 1, No. 1, Oct. 1981, pp. 97–104.

_____. and Hardoy, and Ramirez, R. *Urbanization in Contemporary Latin America.* UK: John Wiley, 1982.

_____. and Ward, P. "Housing in Latin American Cities", in Herbert, and Johnston. (eds). *Geography and the Urban Environment.* USA: John Wiley, 1978, pp. 285–318.

Gough, Ian. *The Political Economy of the Welfare State.* USA: Macmillan, 1979.

Gottschalk, Felix. "A Casa Popular no Sistema Nacional de Habitacao: Um Retrospecto" in *Problemas Brasileiros.* No. 183, Janeiro 1980.

Grant, W. "Dunleavy on Ideological Corporatism: A Comment" in *Public Administration Bulletin.* No. 39, August 1982, pp. 64–66.

Grimes, Oliver. *Housing For Low-Income Urban Families.* Baltimore: John Hopkins University Press, 1976.

Grindle, Merilee. "Patrons and Clients in the Bureaucracy: Career Networks in Mexico" in *Latin American Research Review.* Vol. XII, No. 1, 1977, pp. 37–66.

_____. *Politics and Policy Implementation in the Third World.* USA: Princeton University Press, 1980.

Habermas, Jurgen. *Legitimation Crisis.* London: Heinemann, 1976.

Hardiman, M., and Midgley, J. *The Social Dimensions of Development: Social Policy and Planning in the Third World.* UK: John Wiley, 1982.

Hardoy, J., and Satterthwait, D. *Shelter: Need and Responses.* UK: John Wiley, 1981.

Harrison, G. *Accumulation, Technological Change & Transformation of the Labour Process.* USA: Library of Congress, 1983.

Heady, Bruce. *Housing Policy in the Developed Economy.* London: Croom Helm, 1978.

Heady, Ferrel. *Public Administration: A Comparative Perspective.* New Jersey: Prentice Hall, 1966.

Heidenheimer, Arnold. *Comparative Public Policy.* NY: St. Martins Press, 1983.

Hogwood, Brian. "Policy Analysis: The Danger of Oversophistication" in *Public Administration Bulletin.* UK: No. 44, April 1984, pp. 19–28.

Hoffman, Rodolfo. "Informacoes Necessarias Para a Analise da Distribuicao Pessoul da Renda No Brasil" in *Estudos CEBRAP.* No. 21, Jul/Aug/Set/ 1977, pp. 161–167.

Hughes, Steven, and Mijeski, K. *Politics and Public Policy in Latin America.* USA: Westview Press, 1984.

Huntington, S.P. *Political Order in Changing Societies.* Yale UP, 1968.

Johnson, J. (ed). *The Role of the Military in Underdeveloped Countries.* Princeton UP, 1962.

King, Anthony. "Overload: Problems of Governing in the 1970's" in *Political Studies.* Vol. 23, 1975, pp. 284–296.

Kinzo, M. "The MDB in Sao Paulo" in *Bulletin of Latin American Research.* Vol. 2, 3, July 1984.

Knight, Peter, and Moran, M. *Brazil: Poverty and Basic Needs.* World Bank, Dec. 1981.

Kowarick, Lucio. *Capitalismo e Marginalidade na America Latina.* Brasil: Paz e Terra, 1975.

_____ . *Estrategia do Planejamento Social no Brasil.* S.P.: Cadernos CEBRAP, 1976.

_____ . and Ant, C. "Cortico: Cem Anos de Promiscuidade" in *Novos Estudos —CEBRAP.* Vol. 1, No. 2, Abril 1982, pp. 59–64.

_____ . "The Logic of Disorder: Capitalist Expansion in the Metropolitan Area of Greater Sao Paulo" in *Institute of Development Studies.* Brighton: DP102, University of Sussex, Feb. 1977.

_____ . *A Espoliacao Urbana.* Rio de Janeiro, Paz e Terra, 1980.

Kucinski, B. *Brazil: State & Struggle.* London: LAB, 1982.

Lago, Paulo F. Rocha. "O Regime da Propriedade Imobiliaria" in *Revista de Administracao Municipal.* No. 134, Jan/Fev 1976, pp. 18–30.

Lafer, Betty Mindlin. *Planejamento No Brasil.* Brasil: Editora Perspectiva, 1975.

Le Grand, Julian. *The Strategy of Equality: Redistribution and the Social Services.* London: George Allen & Unwin, 1982.

Leeds, Elizabeth, and Anthony. *Brazil in the 1960's.* LADAC Occasional Papers, Series 2, No. 5, University of Texas, 1972.

_____ . *A Sociologia do Brasil Urbano.* Rio: Zahar Editoras, 1978.

Leff, Nathaniel. *Underdevelopment and Development in Brazil.* London: Allen & Unwin, 1982.

Leff, Nathaniel. *Economic Policy-Making & Development in Brazil*. USA: J. Wiley, 1968.

Lindblom, Charles. *The Policy-Making Process*. NJ: Prentice–Hall, 1980.

Lipset, S., and Solari, A. *Elites in Latin America*. NY: OUP, 1964.

LLoyd, Peter. *A Third World Proletariat?*. UK: George Allen & Unwin, 1982.

———. *The Young Towns of Lima*. UK: Cambridge University Press, 1980.

Love, Joseph. *Sao Paulo in the Brazilian Federation in 1889–1937*. California: Stanford, 1980.

Lowenthal, A. (ed). *Armies and Politics in Latin America*. USA: Holmes & Meir, 1977.

Mabogunje, Akin. "The Case for Big Cities" in *Habitat International*. UK: Vol. 7 No. 5, 1983, pp. 21–31.

Machado da Silva, Luiz. "A Politica na Favela" in *Cadernos Brasileiros*. IX, 41, June 1967, pp. 35–47.

Malloy, James. "Previdencia Social e Classe Operaria no Brasil" in *Estudos CEBRAP*. No. 15, Jan–Mar. 1976, pp. 117–131.

———. *Authoritarianism & Corporatism in Latin America*. USA: Univ. of Pittsburgh Press, 1977.

Mangin, W. "Latin American Squatter Settlements: a Problem and a Solution" in *Latin American Research Review*. 2, 1967, pp. 65–98.

Mangin, W., and Turner, J. "Barriada Movement" in *Progressive Architecture*. 49, 1968, pp. 154–162

Maricato, Erminia. "Autoconstrucao, A Arquitetura Possivel" in Maricato, E. (ed). *A Producao Capitalista da Casa e da Cidade no Brasil Industrial*. Sao Paulo: Editora Alfa-Omega, 1979, pp. 71–93.

Marx, Karl, and Engels, F. *The Communist Manifesto*. UK: Harmondsworth, Penguin Books, 1967.

———. *Capital-I*. London: NLB, 1976.

McDonough, Peter. *Power and Ideology in Brazil*. USA: Princeton University Press, 1981.

———. "Repression and Representation in Brazil" in *Comparative Politics*. Vol. 15, No. 1, Oct. 1982, pp. 73–99.

Medeiros, Antonio Carlos de. *Inter-Governmental Relations in Brazil: The Case of Sao Paulo* Phd, London School of Economics, 1983.

Meehan, Eugene. *The Quality of Federal Policymaking Programmed Failure in Public Housing*. London: University of Missury Press, 1979.

Meirelles, Hely Lopes. "Desapropriacao Para Urbanizacao" in *Revista de Administracao Municipal*. No. 127, Nov/Dez. 1974, pp. 40–56.

———. "As Restricoes de Loteamento e as Leis Urbanisticas" in *Revista de Administracao Municipal*. No. 126, Set./Oct. 1974, pp. 26–37.

Mendonca, Lycia de. "A Political Habitacional a Partir de 1964" in *Revista de Ciencia Politica*. Vol. 23, No. 3, Dez. 1980, pp. 141–161.

Mericle, Kenneth. "Corporatist Control of the Working Class: Authoritarian Brazil Since 1964" in Malloy, James.(ed). *Autoritarianism and Corporatism in Latin America* USA: University of Pittsburgh Press, 1977, pp. 303–337.

Merret, Stephen. *State Housing in Britain*. London: Routledge and Kegan Paul, 1979.

Miliband, R. *The State in Capitalist Society.* UK: Macmillan, 1969.

Misra, R.P., and Dung, Nguyen. "Large Cities: Growth, Dynamics and Emergency Problems" in *Habitat International.*Vol. 7, No. 5/6, pp. 47–65.

Motta, Caio Fabio (ed). *Nivel de Satisfacao em Conjuntos Habitacionais da Grande Sao Paulo.* Vol. 1., S.P.: Instituto de Pesquisas Tecnologicas, 1975.

_____ . *O Papel do BNH no Cenario Socio-Economico Brasileiro pos- . 1964.* S.P.: Instituto de Pesquisas Tecnologicas, 1976.

Munck, R. "The Labour Movement and the Crisis of the Dictatorships in Brazil" in Bruneau, T. *Authoritarian Capitalism.* USA: Westview Press, 1981.

Nickson, Andrew. "The Itaipu Hydro-Electric Project: The Paraguayan Perspective"in *Bulletin of Latin American Research.* UK: Vol. 12, No. 1, Oct. 1982, pp. 1–20.

Nunes, Guida. *Rio, Metropole de 300 Favelas.* Petropolis, Vozes, 1976.

O'Connor, James. *The Fiscal Crisis of the State.* NY: St. Martin's Press, 1973.

O'Donnell, Guillermo. *Modernization & Bureaucratic-Authoritarianism.* USA: Berkley, 1973

_____ . "Reflections on the Patterns of Change in the Bureaucratic-Authoritarian State" in *Latin American Research Review.* Vol. xiii, Nov. 1978, pp. 3–38.

_____ . "Corporatism and the Question of the State" in Malloy, J. *Authoritarianism and Corporatism in Latin America.* USA: Univ. of Pittsburgh Press, 1977, pp. 47–87.

Oliveira, Francisco de. *A Economia Brasileira: Critica a Razao Dualista.* Petropolis: Editora Vozes, 1981.

Pastore, Jose. *Inequality & Social Mobility in Brazil.* USA: Univ. of Wisconsin Press, 1982.

Pereira, Luis Bresser. *Pactos Politicos.* S.P.: Brasiliense, 1985.

_____ . *Desenvolvimento e Crise no Brasil.* S.P.: Brasiliense, 1983.

Perlman, Janice. "The Failure of Influence: Squatter Eradication in Brazil", in Greendale, Merilee. *Politics & Policy Implementation.* USA: Princeton University Press, 1980, pp. 250–280.

Perlman, Janice. *The Myth of Marginality: Urban Poverty and Politics in Rio.* USA: University of California Press, 1976.

Peruzzo, Silvo. *Habitacao: Controle e Espoliacao.* S.P.: Cortez Editora, 1984.

Peters, Guy. *The Politics of Bureaucracy.* NY: Longman, 1978.

Philip, George. "The Military Institutions Revisited" in *Journal of Latin American Studies.* 12, No. 2, November 1980.

Philip, George. "Military Rule in South America" in Clapham, C., and Philip, G. *Political Dilemmas of Military Regimes.* UK: Croom Helm, 1984.

_____ . "Military Authoritarianism in South America" in *Political Studies.* Vol. 22, No. 1, March 1984, pp. 1–20.

_____ . "The Fall of the Argentine Military" in *Third World Quarterly.* Vol. 6., No. 3, July 1984.

_____ . "Democratization in Brazil & Argentina" in *Government & Opposition.* Vol. 19, No. 2, 1984, pp. 269–276.

_____ . *The Military in South American Politics.* UK: Croom Helm, 1985.

Pickvance, C. *Urban Sociology: Critical Essays.* London: Tavistock, 1976.

Portes, Alejandro. "Housing Policy, Urban Poverty and the State" in *Latin American Research Review.* Vol. xiv, No. 2, 1979, pp. 3–24.

———. "Politica Habitacional,Pobreza Urbana e o Estado" in *Estudos CE-BRAP.* No. 22, 1978, pp. 133–161.

Poulantzas, N. *The Crisis of Dictatorship.* London: NLB, 1976.

Poulantzas, N. *Political Power & Social Classes.* London: NLB, 1973.

Pressman, Jeffrey, and Wildavsky, A. *Implementation.* Berkley: University of California Press, 1979.

Rattner, Henrique. *Planejamento Urbano e Regional.* Brasil: Editora Nacional, 1978.

Rein, Martin. *Social Science and Public Policy.* UK: Penguin Books, 1976.

———. *Social Policy: Issues of Choice & Change.* NY: Random House, 1970.

Renaud, Bertrand. *National Urbanization Policy in Developing Countries.* OUP, 1981.

Reynolds, Clark, and Carpenter, R. "Financiamento a Habitacao e Distribuicao de Riqueza no Brasil" in *Revista de Administracao de Empresas.* FGV: Vol. 17, No. 5, Set/Out. 1977, pp. 43–61.

Roberts, Bryan. *Cities of Peasants.* UK: Edward Arnolds, 1981.

Roett, Riordan. *Brazil—Politics in a Patrimonial Society.* NY: Praeger, 1978.

Romani, Carlos. "O Deficit Habitacional no Estado do Rio" in *Revista de Administracao Municipal.* Abril/Junho 1978, pp. 38–48.

Rourke, Francis. *Bureaucracy, Politics & Public Policy.* Boston: Little Brown & Co., 1976.

Rose, Richard. *Do Parties Make a Difference?* Macmillan Press, 1984.

———. and Peters, G. *Can Government Go Bankrupt?.* UK: Macmillan Press, 1979.

Roxborough, Ian. *Theories of Underdevelopment.* London: Macmillan, 1979.

Sandilands, Roger. *Monetary Correction & Housing Finance in Colombia, Brazil and Chile.* UK: Gower, 1980.

Santos, Nelson dos, and Bronstein, O. "Metaurbanizacao—O Caso do Rio de Janeiro" in *Revista de Administracao Municipal.* No. 149, Oct/Dez 1978, pp. 6–34.

Sarles, Margaret. "Maintaining Political Control Through Parties" in *Comparative Politics.* Vol. 5, No. 1, Oct. 1982, pp. 41–72.

Saunders, Peter. *Urban Politics—A Sociological Interpretation.* London: Hutchinson, 1984.

Schaffer, Bernard, and Lamb, G. *Can Equity be Organized?* UK: Gower Press, 1981.

Schmidt, Benicio. *O Estado e a Politica Urbana no Brasil.* Porte Alegre: Editora da Universidade, 1983.

Schmitter, P. *Interest, Conflict & Political Change in Brazil.* USA: Stanford, UP., 1971.

Schneider, Ronald. *The Political System of Brazil.* USA: Columbia University Press, 1971.

Schulman, Mauricio. "A Ideologia Oficial do Desenvolvimento Urbano" in *Revista de Administracao Municipal.* No. 151, Abr/Jun 1979, pp. 61–74.

Schwartzman, Simon. "Back to Weber: Corporatism & Patrimonialism in the 1970's" in Malloy, J. (ed). *Authoritarianism & Corporatism in Latin America.* USA: University of Pittsburgh Press, 1977, pp. 89–106.

Schwartzman, Simon. *Bases do Autoritarismo Brasileiro.* Brasil: Campus, 1982.

––––––. *Sao Paulo e o Estado Nacional.* Sao Paulo, 1975.

Self, Peter. *Administrative Theories & Politics.* London: Allen & Unwin, 1979.

––––––. *Planning the Urban Region.* London: Allen & Unwin, 1982.

––––––. *Political Theories of Modern Government.* London: Allen & Unwin, 1985.

Serran, Joao. *O IAB e a Politica Habitacional Brasileira.* Brasil: Schema, 1976.

Shidlo, Gil. *An Analysis of Political Corruption in Developing Countries* Unpublished MSc. Dissertation, London School of Economics, 1983.

––––––. *Housing Policy in Developing Countries.* London: Routledge, 1990.

––––––. "Budgetary Trends in Military Regimes"in *Journal of Interdisciplinary Economics* University of Exeter, Vol. 2, No. 4, 1988.

––––––. "Notes on Recent Elections: The Brazilian Elections of November 1986" in *World Review* Forthcoming.

––––––. "The Brazilian National Housing Bank: End of An Era?" New Delhi: *Fourth International Congress On Human Settlements In Developing Countries,* 1988.

Singer, Paul. "O Uso do Solo Urbano na Economia Capitalista" in Maricato, E. *A Producao Capitalista da Casa e da Cidade no Brasil Industrial.* S.P.: Editora Alfa Omega, 1979, pp. 21–93.

Singer, Paul. "Urbanizacao e Desenvolvimento: O Caso de Sao Paulo" in *CEBRAP.* Caderno No. 14, 1973, pp. 67–90.

Skidmore, Thomas. *Politics in Brazil.* OUP, 1976.

––––––. *Brasil: De Getulio a Castelo.* RJ: Paz e Terra, 1982.

––––––. and Smith, P. *Modern Latin America.* USA: OUP, 1984.

Souza, Bernice. *O BNH e a Politica do Governo.* MA Thesis, UFMG, 1974.

Steinberg, Florian. "Slum and the Shanty Upgrading in Colombia" in *International Journal of Urban & Regional Studies.* Vol. 6, No. 3, Sept. 1982, pp. 372–392.

Stepan, Alfred. *The Military in Politics: Changing Patterns in Brazil.* USA: Princeton UP, 1971.

––––––.(ed). *Authoritarian Brazil.* USA: Yale UP, 1973.

––––––. *The State and Society.* UK: Princeton University Press, 1978.

Stretton, Hugh. *Urban Planning in Rich and Poor Countries.* UK: OUP, 1978.

Swerdlow, I. *Development Administration Concepts & Problems.* Syracuse: Syracuse University Press, 1963.

Taschner, Suzana Pasternak. "Favelas do Municipio de Sao Paulo" in Blay, Eva (ed). *A Luta Pelo Espaco.* Petropolis: Vozes, 1978, pp. 125–147.

Taylor, John, and Williams, D.(ed). *Urban Planning Practice in Developing Countries.* UK: Pergamon Press, 1982.

Trinidade, Mario. *Housing and Urban Development.* RJ: BNH, 1971.

Valladares, Licia. *Housing in Brazil: An Introduction to Recent Literature.* Paper Presented at the 10th World Congress of Sociology, Mexico, 1982.

———. "Working the System: Squatter Response to Resettlement in Rio" in *International Journal of Urban & Regional Studies.* Vol. 12, No. 1, 1978, pp. 12–25.

———. "Favela, Politica e Conjunto Residencial" in *DADOS.* RJ: IUPERJ, No. 12, 1976, pp. 74–85.

———. "A Proposito da Urbanizacao de Favelas" in *Espaco e Debates.* Maio 1981, pp. 5–18.

———.(ed). *Repensando a Habitacao no Brasil.* RJ: Zahar, 1982.

———. *Passa-se Uma Casa.* RJ: Zahar, 1980.

———. *Habitacao em Questao.* RJ: Zahar, 1981.

Vetter, David. "Uso do Solo e Distribuicao da Renda" in *Revista de Administracao Municipal.* No. 133, Nov/Dez 1975, pp. 23–35.

———. "Politica de Uso de Solo: Para Quem?" in *Revista de Administracao Municipal.* Oct/Dez 1979, pp. 7–31.

Viana, Luis Filho. *O Governo Castelo Branco.* Brasil: Jose Olympia, 1975.

Ward, Peter. "Mexico City" in Pacione, M. (ed). *Problems & Planning in Third World Cities.* UK: Croom Helm, 1981.

Weffort, Francisco. *O Populismo na Politica Brasileira.* Brasil: Paz e Terra, 1978.

Werneck, Dorothea. *Emprego e Salarios na Industria de Construcao.* RJ: IPEA, 1978

Wildavsky, Aaron. *Speaking Truth to Power: The Art & Craft of Policy Analysis.* Boston: Little Brown & Co., 1979.

Wilheim, Jorge. *Projeto Sao Paulo.* Brasil: Paz e Terra, 1982.

Wynia, Gary. *The Politics of Latin American Development.* USA: CUP, 1984.

Zirker, Daniel. "Brazilian Development" in *Latin American Research Review.* Vol. XVIII, No. 2, 1983, pp. 135–149.

Periodical Publications

Anuario Estatistico do Estado de Sao Paulo, Sao Paulo.

Anuario Estatistico do Brasil, Sao Paulo: FIBGE.

BNH Annual Reports, Rio de Janeiro.

COHAB/Sao Paulo Annual Reports, Sao Paulo.

CODESPAULO Annual Reports, Sao Paulo.

Construcao Sao Paulo, Sao Paulo.

Folha de Sao Paulo, Sao Paulo.

Governo do Estado de Sao Paulo/Reports, Sao Paulo: Secretaria de Economia e Planejamento.

Governo do Municipio de Sao Paulo/Budgets, Sao Paulo: Secretaria das Financas.

INOCOOP/Sao Paulo Annual Reports, Sao Paulo.

Journal do Brasil, Rio de Janeiro.

Journal da Tarde, Sao Paulo.

Latin America, London.

Latin American Economic Report, London.
Latin American Newsletters, London.
O Estado de Sao Paulo, London.
Sinopse Preliminar do Censo Demografico do Brasil, Sao Paulo: FIBGE, 1980.
Sinopse Preliminar do Censo Demografico de Sao Paulo, Sao Paulo: FIBGE, 1980.
World Bank, Annual Report, Washington, D.C.
Veja, Sao Paulo.

Interviews

Approximately twenty interviews were conducted between October 1983 and March 1984 with officials from the National Housing Bank; COHAB/Sao Paulo; CODESPAULO; INOCOOP; The Brazilian Institute of Technology (Housing Division); Sao Paulo Secretary of Housing; Sao Paulo Secretary of Planning; and various Brazilian academics. Since interviewees were promised that their names and institutions would not be revealed, their identification is withheld by the author.

Index